2·55

By the same author
Patterns in Physics

Physical science for technicians
A first level unit

W. Bolton
Advisory Officer, Technician Education Council

McGRAW-HILL Book Company (UK) Limited

London · New York · St Louis · San Francisco · Auckland · Bogotá
Düsseldorf · Johannesburg · Madrid · Mexico · Montreal · New Delhi
Panama · Paris · São Paulo · Singapore · Sydney · Tokyo · Toronto

Published by
McGRAW-HILL Book Company (UK) Limited
MAIDENHEAD · BERKSHIRE · ENGLAND

Library of Congress Cataloging in Publication Data

Bolton, William Charles.
  Physical science for technicians.

  Includes Bibliographies and index.
  1. Physics. I. Title.
QC23.B6858   530   76–26552
ISBN 0–07–084216–7

12345 W&JM 79876

PRINTED IN GREAT BRITAIN

Contents

Introduction

This book has been designed to meet the needs of technicians studying a first level Physical Science unit in programmes leading to the certificate and diploma awards of the Technician Education Council. The objectives listed in the Technician Education Council Physical Science unit TEC U75/004 are covered. In fact, the book covers more than the objectives in that unit, and so might be appropriate for many first level units of a similar form.

The following is a list of the general objectives that the book is designed to cover; the references in brackets alongside the objectives refer to the related general objective references in the unit TEC U75/004. General objectives, within the form adopted by the Technician Education Council, give the main teaching goals. The specific objectives are not given here, these being the means by which the student demonstrates his attainment of the general objectives. All the objectives below should be considered to be prefixed by words such as 'The expected learning outcome is that the student...'.

Chapter 1

1. Describes the relationship between mass and volume for a substance, and defines the term density (A1).
2. Recognizes in words, graphs, and equations, what is meant by the term 'proportional to'.
3. Describes the effect of forces on materials (A2).
4. Describes the structure of matter in terms of atomic building blocks (A3).
5. Distinguishes between compounds and mixtures, compounds and elements (A3).
6. Uses SI units and the common multiples and submultiples of those units (D10).

Chapter 2

7. Solves problems involving forces in static equilibrium situations (F16).

Chapter 3

8. Solves straight line motion problems involving uniform speed or uniform acceleration (E14).
9. Recognizes an acceleration as being the result of a net force (E14).

10. Describes energy and its transformations (B4).
11. Describes and calculates frictional forces between two surfaces in contact (E15).

Chapter 4

12. Defines pressure and calculates pressures in static fluids (F17).
13. Explains and measures atmospheric pressure (F17).

Chapter 5

14. Measures temperature (B5).
15. Defines and solves problems involving specific heat capacity (B6).
16. Describes changes of state and solves problems involving specific latent heats (B6).
17. Describes the effects of heat (B8).
18. Describes the transfer of heat (B7).

Chapter 6

19. Assembles simple series and parallel circuits and solves problems involving V, I, and R (D10).
20. Defines resistivity and solves problems involving resistivity (I22).
21. Describes the effects of currents (F11).
22. Defines power and solves electrical problems involving power (F12).
23. Describes the concepts of e.m.f. and internal resistance (I23).
24. Describes the magnetic field concept and the relationships between magnetic fields and electric currents (F13).
25. Describes the production of charge by friction.

Chapter 7

26. Describes waves and their properties of reflection and refraction (C9).
27. Describes the basic properties of sound (C9).
28. Describes the basic properties of light (H21).

Chapter 8

29. Describes oxidation (G18).
30. Describes and explains the conduction of electricity through solutions (G19).
31. Describes the production of electricity from chemical reactions (G19).
32. Distinguishes between acids and alkalis (G20).
33. Explains the concept of a chemical equation (G20).

W. BOLTON
1976

1. Materials

1.1 The diversity of materials

Look around you at the different materials used. The window frames might be wood or metal; the walls might be brick or reinforced concrete; there are probably some plastics items. The material chosen for a particular item will depend on what job that item is to do. What is the best material for carrying electricity? What is the best material for the bodywork of a car? Over the years new materials have been developed, and what might have been the best material at one particular time might not be the best available at some later time. What are the properties which enable us to decide the 'best' for some particular purpose?

This chapter looks at some of the properties of materials which can enable us to make some of the decisions towards deciding the 'best'; later chapters will give yet more information about the properties.

Without working through this chapter, you might like to consider what you feel are the reasons for car bodies being predominantly made of steel. Why steel? Why not wood? Why not a plastics material? Steel first started being used for car bodies in the year 1912; the first glass-reinforced plastics saloon car body was produced in 1953. What do you think will be the material used for car bodies in the year 2000? This assumes that we will still have cars in that year. At the end of this chapter, and at later stages in your course, you might like to consider how your answers to these questions will change.

1.2 Density and mass

If you pick up a one centimetre cube of wood and then a one centimetre cube of iron you can easily tell the difference—the iron is heavier than the wood. Though the two blocks have the same volume they have different masses. We say that iron is denser than wood. The amount of mass per unit volume is called the density.

$$\text{density} = \frac{\text{mass}}{\text{volume}}$$

The volume of a cube is the side length cubed, i.e., length × length × length, so that a cube with sides of length 1 centimetre (cm) has a volume of 1 cubic centimetre (cm³). The block of wood might have a mass of 0·7 grammes and so the density would be 0·7 grammes per cm³. The iron block might have a

1

mass of 7·9 grammes and so would have a density of 7·9 grammes per cm³. The iron has a higher density than the wood. The density of the iron is more than ten times that of the wood, and so, for identical volumes of iron and wood, the iron block will have a mass more than ten times that of the wooden block.

Suppose we have, in one hand, a 1 cm cube of wood and, in the other hand, another cube of wood but this time the sides of the cube have lengths of 2 cm instead of the 1 cm. Which block would be the heavier? The obvious answer is the bigger block. But how much heavier? The volume of a cube with sides of length 2 cm is $2 \times 2 \times 2 = 8$ cm³. If you used a balance to measure the mass of this bigger cube, the result obtained would be about 5·6 g. The following table gives the results of an experiment in which different blocks of wood had their volumes determined from measurements of the lengths of their sides, and their masses measured using a balance.

| Mass in grammes | 0 | 0·7 | 5·6 | 18·9 |
| Volume in cm³ | 0 | 1 | 8 | 27 |

The greater the volume of a cube the greater the mass. If the volume is increased by a factor of eight, i.e., from 1 cm³ to 8 cm³, then the mass increases from 0·7 grammes to 5·6 grammes. But $8 \times 0.7 = 5.6$. Increasing the volume by a factor of eight has increased the mass by a factor of eight.

If the volume is increased by a factor of 27, i.e., from 1 cm³ to 27 cm³, then the mass increases from 0·7 grammes to 18·9 grammes. But $27 \times 0.7 = 18.9$. Increasing the volume by a factor of twenty-seven has increased the mass by a factor of twenty-seven.

We say that the mass is *proportional to* the volume. This can be written as

$$\text{mass} \propto \text{volume}$$

$\propto$ is the sign used to mean 'proportional to'. The mass being proportional to the volume means that if we have double the volume we must have double the mass. If we have treble the volume we must have treble the mass. By whatever factor we increase the volume we must increase the mass by the same factor. Mass thus seems to be the term applied to indicate the 'quantity of matter' in a body. The bigger the body the greater the quantity of matter present and so the greater the mass.

You might in the laboratory have measured the mass of an object by using a balance. This could have the form of what is essentially a beam pivoted at its centre; Fig. 1.1. The unknown mass is suspended from one end of the beam and, at the other end, an equal distance from the pivot point, calibrated masses are placed. When the pivoted beam resumes its initial horizontal position it is assumed that the object has a mass equal to the known mass at the other end of the beam.

The units of mass are grammes. A kilogramme is a thousand grammes. Instead of writing out the word grammes in full every time the unit is written the abbreviation g is used. Thus 20 grammes would be written as 20 g. The abbreviation for kilogrammes is kg. Thus 4 kilogrammes is written as 4 kg.

A beam balance, like that shown in Fig. 1.1, or a spring balance, actually measures the gravitational forces acting on the masses. You can, however, accept as an experimental fact that the gravitational force is proportional to the mass. If a block of wood has twice the gravitational force of a '1 kg mass' then its mass will be twice that of '1 kg', i.e., it will have a mass of 2 kg.

Fig. 1.1 A simple balance (courtesy Griffin and George Ltd)

1.3 Graphs

The following are data showing how the masses of blocks of the same wood are related to their volumes.

Mass in grammes	0	0·7	1·4	2·1	2·8
Volume in cm³	0	1	2	3	4

The mass is directly proportional to the volume. If the volume is doubled the mass doubles.

There are many examples in science, and elsewhere, where changing one thing results in another thing changing. In this case, changing the volume changes the mass. There is a relationship between the one set of quantities and the other. With a volume of 1 cm³ we link a mass of 0·7 g. With a volume of 2 cm³ we link a mass of 1·4 g. Figure 1.2 shows the links between the two sets of data.

There is another way of showing the relationship between two sets of data,

3

and that is by means of a graph. To find a point on a map it is convenient to refer, for example, to the distance the point is east of some origin and the distance it is north of the same origin; Fig. 1.3. These two distances, e.g., 3 km east and 5 km north, give what are called the coordinates of the point.

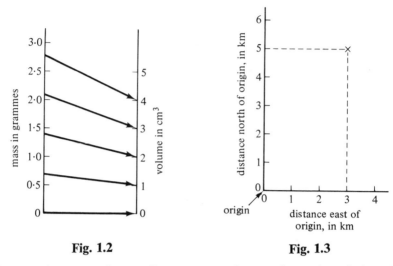

Fig. 1.2   Fig. 1.3

The map has two reference lines, one running north–south and the other east–west. These are called axes. To find the point referred to, we need to move 3 km along the east–west axis in an easterly direction from the origin, and then north a distance of 5 km. In the case of our relationship between mass and volume we would represent the axes as mass and volume scales; Fig. 1.4. To find the point representing the volume of 1 cm³ and mass 0·7 g we would move, from the origin, a distance related to a volume of 1 cm³ and then in a direction at right-angles a distance related to a mass of 0·7 g. The resulting position is then taken to represent 1 cm³ volume having 0·7 g mass. The complete graph for the volume–mass data, given in Fig. 1.4, is a straight line passing through the origin. This is always the case where the two quantities are directly proportional.

1.4 Force

We might describe forces as pushes and pulls. If somebody pushes or pulls you, we can say they are applying forces to you. If you pull a spring between your hands we can say that your hands are applying forces to the ends of the spring. A spring balance measures forces. Spring balances are given scales: grammes, kilogrammes or perhaps newtons. Grammes and kilogrammes are units of mass. A spring balance measures the gravitational force acting on a mass, and because this force is directly proportional to the mass we tend to ignore the conversion factor and just calibrate the scale in terms of the mass. Thus when the balance indicates, say, 10 g it means that the balance is recording the force that a 10 g mass experiences when subject to gravitational forces, near the surface of the Earth. If we wish to record the results as a force it is convenient to call the force 10 g force, 10 gf. A spring balance recording say 2 kg is really recording the force on 2 kg due to gravity, i.e., 2 kgf. The unit of force is the newton (N). A force of one newton is approximately the gravitational force experienced by a 100 g mass at the surface of the Earth. Thus 1 N is about 100 gf. In a later chapter the reason for this conversion will be dealt with and the more exact factor considered. The newton is actually defined as the force required to give a mass of 1 kg an acceleration of 1 metre per second.

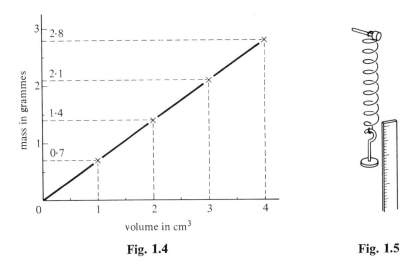

Fig. 1.4   Fig. 1.5

1.5 Stretching and compressing

If you pull at the two ends of a strip of rubber it stretches; if you press a block of rubber between your fingers, an eraser for example, it becomes compressed. When the rubber stretches it increases in length, when it is compressed it becomes shorter. We talk of the rubber being under tension when it is stretched and under compression when compressed. We can stretch, or we can compress, many things: pieces of rubber, springs, blocks of concrete metal rods, blocks of wood, pieces of plastic, etc. A knowledge of the stretching and compressing properties of materials is relevant to an understanding of the behaviour of materials in use. Rubber stretches more easily than aluminium—what would it be like if aeroplanes had fuselages built of rubber and not aluminium?

Suppose we take a spring, hook one end over a nail and then attach masses to the lower end (Fig. 1.5): the spring stretches. If we clamp a rule alongside the spring we can measure how much the spring stretches when the masses

5

are attached. The following might be the type of results obtained if you did the experiment:

Load in g	0	50	100	150	200	250
Extension in cm	0	1·9	4·0	6·0	7·9	10·1

A 50 g load produces an extension of 1·9 cm; twice the load, 100 g, gives an extension of 4·0 cm. Twice the load has produced about twice the extension. Three times the load gives about three times the extension. The extension is proportional to the load.

$$\text{extension} \propto \text{load}$$

Figure 1.6 shows the above results as a graph. Because the graph is a straight line passing through the zero load, zero extension point this informs us that the extension is proportional to the load. The statement 'extension is proportional to the applied load' is known as *Hooke's law* (obtained in 1676).

If we had applied very large loads to the spring we would have found that the extension, beyond some particular load value, ceased to become proportional to the load. The spring also ceases to be elastic, that is when the load is removed the spring no longer returns to its original dimension, but remains permanently elongated. Many materials obey Hooke's law up to this *elastic limit*.

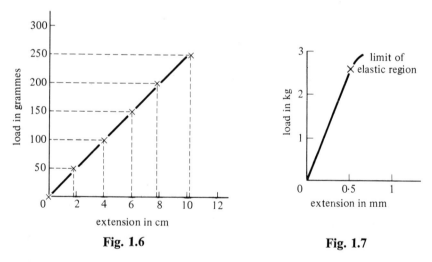

Fig. 1.6   Fig. 1.7

Figure 1.7 shows a load–extension graph for a bar of cast iron. The iron obeys Hooke's law up to the elastic limit. In fact, the iron cannot be extended much beyond the elastic limit before it breaks. This makes it difficult to give cast iron permanent deformation without breaking it. If we want to bend a bar of cast iron without breaking it, but so that when we release the load the bar remains bent, then we have to apply loads which stretch the iron to values falling between the elastic limit and the breaking point. Cast iron is considered a *brittle* material because it does not significantly deform.

6

Figure 1.8 shows a load–extension graph for a strip of rubber. The rubber obeys Hooke's law only for quite small loads, loads far below the elastic limit. The elastic limit for rubber is nowhere near the limit of proportionality, i.e., the end of the initial straight line part of the graph. Rubber can be stretched a very long way and still return to its original dimensions when released. Rubber is what we call an *elastic* material.

Figure 1.9 shows a load–extension graph for a piece of copper. The copper obeys Hooke's law initially. There is, however, quite a significant part of the

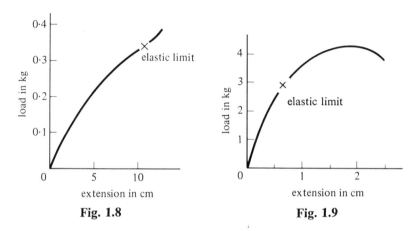

Fig. 1.8   **Fig. 1.9**

load–extension graph beyond the elastic limit. Copper is, thus, more easily bent into permanent shapes than the cast iron. A material which can be given quite large permanent deformations before it breaks is said to be *ductile*.

China is a brittle material, and there is virtually no deformation prior to fracture, so that, if you drop a china cup and it breaks, it is possible to take all the pieces and stick them together again. The elastic limit is almost the same as the breaking point. If a car is hit by another car the wing of the car may just be pushed out of shape, i.e., deformed. By hammering, the wing can be bent back to its original shape. The steel of the bodywork of the car is ductile, quite a lot of deformation being possible before breaking occurs.

The elastic limit and the limit of proportionality are not the same thing and, in general, they are not the same point on a load–extension graph.

1.6 The structure of solids

Metals, wood, plastics, crystals such as those of common salt, all look different in appearance, but scientists believe that they are all built up of basic building blocks called atoms. Liquids and gases are also built up of atoms. We can represent this view of the atom as being comparable to that of the common brick used in constructing buildings. Many different buildings can be produced from tne same building block. But what evidence have we that solids have a structure, that they are built up from building blocks?

Crystals, for example those of sugar or common salt, have flat surfaces and adopt some regular format. Common salt crystals are all basically cubes. When a substance crystallizes, i.e., solidifies from the liquid, all the crystals are of one kind, or possibly just a few related kinds. If you allow a concentrated solution of common salt to evaporate, then the resulting crystals will have the same form as crystals obtained from other sources. When you allow a lot of crystals to grow in a confined space they may not have room to grow into any definite form; however, they will always show the same angle between next-door faces, when you compare one crystal with another.

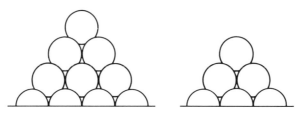

Fig. 1.10

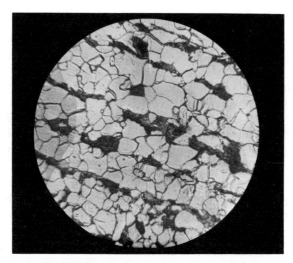

Fig. 1.11   Etched surface of a metal

What has the form of crystals to do with the concept of atoms? We can make sense of this if we consider all crystals to be made up of building blocks. The common salt crystals can be of different sizes, but they still have the same form. We can explain this by considering that in the salt crystal we always build up with the same building blocks in the same way. It is like stacking up oranges in a pile. However big the pile, its form will always be the same, if we keep on packing the oranges together in an orderly manner in the same way. Figure 1.10 shows possible *crystals* arrived at by packing *oranges*.

8

How big could the building blocks be? If you look at a crystal you cannot see the individual blocks; therefore, they must certainly be smaller than a millimetre across. If you use a microscope, the crystal surface still looks smooth; therefore, they must certainly be less than a hundredth of a millimetre. (A human hair is about one-tenth of a millimetre in diameter.) With an electron microscope some detail does become apparent. The evidence points to the building blocks being of the order of a ten-millionth of a millimetre in size, i.e. about

$$\frac{1}{10\ 000\ 000\ 000}\ \text{metre}$$

You can obtain for yourself some evidence for this type of figure. Camphor oil and other similar chemicals float on water, and when a drop of camphor oil is placed on the water it spreads out into a very thin layer. From a measurement of the volume of the oil drop and the area of the layer of the oil when spread out on the water surface the thickness of the oil film can be calculated.

$$\text{volume of drop} = \text{area of film} \times \text{film thickness}$$

The oil on the water surface spreads out, but only so far and no further. It is as though a container of ball bearings had been upturned and the balls spread out in all directions, but only until the layer of balls is just one ball high and only with the resulting layer having all balls in contact with next-door balls. It is as though there were some bonds between the balls which are weak enough to let the balls spread out but not so weak as to allow the balls to escape completely. The results of such experiments confirm the ten-millionth of a millimeter size as being realistic.

If crystals are made up of building blocks, arranged in an orderly way, what is the situation in metals? If metal surfaces are carefully etched, the pattern seen is just like that produced when salt crystals grow in a restricted space. Figure 1.11 shows such a pattern for a metal. The etching process removes the softest parts of the surface and leaves holes which trace out the structure. Metals are crystalline.

The behaviour of other materials, e.g., glass, wood, or plastics, can be explained in terms of building blocks. In the crystals and the metals, we have been considering that the building blocks are atoms. In many substances the basic block is more complex than an atom; it consists of a number of atoms linked together. These building blocks, made up of atoms, are called molecules. The nylon molecule consists of atoms of nitrogen, hydrogen, carbon, and oxygen strung together. The rubber molecule consists of carbon and hydrogen atoms. Both the nylon and rubber molecules are long chains of atoms, and when these materials are stretched their tangled molecules are uncoiled. This is easier to do than trying to pull atoms apart from their next-door atoms, and for this reason, both nylon and rubber are easily stretched.

9

1.7 Compounds and mixtures

Suppose I were to put iron filings in water. I stir them around. After a while I look at the beaker with its contents and find—readily identifiable iron filings in water. If I pour the beaker's content through a filter paper (Fig. 1.12) the two separate to give me iron filings and water.

Suppose I were to put a small quantity of common salt in water. I stir them around. After a while I look at the beaker with its contents and find— a liquid. I cannot see the salt and the water as two separate entities. If I pour the beaker's contents through a filter paper I fail to separate the salt from the water. We talk of the salt being in solution. The iron and the water were just a mixture or a suspension. Suspensions can be separated by *filtration*.

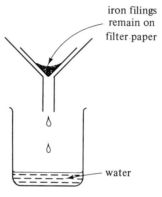

iron filings
remain on
filter paper

water

Fig. 1.12

If I want to extract salt from an impure sample, perhaps a piece of rock salt, I can put the rock salt in water. The salt will dissolve in the water but the sand, that is often around in the rock salt, does not dissolve. The salt can thus be separated from the sand. There may be other substances in the rock salt which are soluble, i.e., dissolve, in the water and so all I can say as the result of such an experiment is that the soluble substances can be separated from the insoluble substances.

How can we separate the salt from the water in which it is dissolved? If the solution is heated the water evaporates. The result of this is that the volume of the solution decreases. The solution tastes salty, but the liquid which evaporates off does not. Figure 1.13 shows a method by which the liquid which evaporates off can be collected. The process is called *distillation*. At the end of such distillation the salt and the water are completely separated again, the salt remaining in the heated vessel and the water being collected in a colder vessel.

The iron filings in the water, and the salt in the water, are what are called mixtures. Filtration and distillation can be used to separate mixtures. Air is a mixture of a number of gases, notably oxygen and nitrogen. To live we have to breathe in oxygen; our body is able to separate the nitrogen and the oxygen. Water contains oxygen and hydrogen but if you put your head under water you cannot live because your body is unable to separate the oxygen from the water. Hydrogen and oxygen at room temperatures are gases, water is not. A *mixture* of two gases is still a gas, having the properties of its constituents in proportion to their relative quantities. Hence we can use the oxygen in air. Water, however, is a liquid although the hydrogen and oxygen which form water are both gases at room temperature. The properties of water bear no relation to the properties of the two gases. Water is what is called a *compound*. Compounds are distinct items with properties all of their own.

In case you wonder how fishes get their oxygen—they do not break down the water to get at the oxygen but depend on the small amount of oxygen that is dissolved in water. This is why in a fish tank you have to put plants or bubble air through the water.

Common salt is a compound. We can eat salt with no harm. Salt is however constituted from chlorine, a poisonous gas, and sodium, a very reactive substance which cannot be kept in air but has to be kept under oil to stop it reacting with the oxygen in the air.

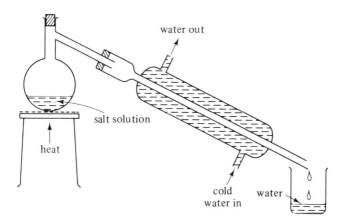

Fig. 1.13

1.8 Elements

Pure salt can be obtained from rock salt by dissolving the rock salt in water and then evaporating the solution down. If we take the resulting residue and redissolve the substance again in water and repeat the experiment we still end up with salt. No matter how many times the experiment is done the result is still salt.

Water is a compound. We can heat it and collect the steam and find that the condensed steam is still water. We can, however, break water down into

11

two other substances, hydrogen and oxygen. We can combine oxygen and hydrogen and make them turn from a mixture of gases into water. The use of heat or electricity enables us to break down compounds. There is a limit to the breaking down; we cannot break oxygen down into other substances by chemical means. We cannot break hydrogen down into other substances by chemical means. The term *element* is used for those substances which cannot be broken down into further substances by chemical means. In certain situations, such as in nuclear reactions, elements can be changed but not by ordinary chemical means.

Examples of elements are hydrogen, oxygen, nitrogen, copper, iron, aluminium, and carbon.

1.9 Solutions

If we put a small amount of common salt in water and stir the two, then we can get the salt to dissolve in the water. If, however, we put a large amount of salt in the water then no matter for how long we stir all the salt will not dissolve in the water. There is a limit to the amount of salt we can dissolve in the water. The water which has dissolved as much salt as it can is said to be *saturated*. The term *solubility* is used for the amount of the salt that can be dissolved in a certain quantity of water. We can express this as so many grammes of salt per 100 g of water.

The amount we can dissolve in water depends on the temperature of the solution. The higher the temperature the more salt can be dissolved, i.e., the greater the solubility. At 0°C we can dissolve 35·7 g of salt in 100 g of water; at 20°C the amount is 36·0 g; and at 100°C it is 39·8 g. The amount that can be dissolved at a particular temperature depends on the two substances involved. In beers and spirits alcohol is dissolved in water. Liquid copper will dissolve in nickel; the result is an alloy. On cooling down, back to the solid state, the two constituents do not separate out. The result is then called a *solid solution*.

1.10 Atoms and molecules

The building blocks of matter are the atoms. We thus have atoms of hydrogen, atoms of oxygen, atoms of copper, etc. Compounds, however, are built up of different elements, water being, for example, atoms of hydrogen with oxygen. We do not refer to atoms of water but use the word molecule— a molecule of water. The molecule of water is made up of hydrogen and oxygen atoms. Hydrogen itself, in the gaseous form, does not usually exist as just single hydrogen atoms but as a molecule involving two hydrogen atoms linked together. Some atoms can exist singly, but most tend to exist in groups, i.e., molecules.

Appendix: Units

The International System (SI) of units is used in this book. On this system, the units of quantities are specified in terms of a set of basic units:

Length in metres; symbol of unit m

Mass in kilogrammes; symbol kg

Time in seconds; symbol s

Electric current in amperes; symbol A

and also temperature and luminous intensity

Multiples and sub-multiples of these units are shown by prefixes to the units. The more common prefixes are:

mega, a million times; symbol M

kilo, a thousand times; symbol k

centi, a hundredth; symbol c

milli, a thousandth, symbol m

micro, a millionth, symbol μ

Thus a kilometre, km, is a thousand metres; a millimetre, mm, is a thousandth of a metre.

The following are some further interpretations of the above prefixes with imaginary units (taken from *The NBS Standard*, **15**, 1 January 1970 by P. A. Simson).

a million phones = 1 megaphone

a hundredth of a pede = 1 centipede

a thousandth of an ink machine = 1 millink machine

a millionth of a phone = 1 microphone

You might like to think of some 'units' of your own!

Problems

The diversity of materials

1. Identify the types of materials, i.e., plastics, metal, etc., used in the construction of one of the following:
   (a) a modern house,
   (b) a modern office block,
   (c) a house built at least a hundred years ago.
2. What type of properties do you think are important in the selection of the material used to make:
   (a) a desk top,
   (b) a washing-up bowl for the kitchen,
   (c) electric overhead cables?

Density and mass

3. A cube has sides of length 2 cm. What is the volume of the cube?
4. The density of iron is 7·9 g per cm³. What is:
   (a) the mass of an iron block of volume 4 cm³,
   (b) the volume of an iron block of mass 15·8 g?

5. A builder orders 2 m³ of sand. The density of dry sand is 1·6 g per cm³, i.e., 1·6 million g per m³. What is the mass of the sand, assuming it is dry?

6. Comparing a 1 kg bag full of feathers and a 1 kg bag full of lead, what will be the greater for the lead—the mass, the volume, the density?

7. On the basis of the following data decide if the cost of oranges is proportional to the number of oranges bought:

Number	0	2	4	6	8	10
Cost in units of currency	0	4	8	12	16	20

8. On the basis of the following data decide if the total cost for entrance to a theatre is proportional to the number in the party:

Number	0	4	8	12	16	20
Cost in units of currency	0	100	200	275	375	450

9. Describe the sequence of operations you would use when employing a simple beam balance to determine the mass of an object.

Graphs

10. Plot graphs of the data given in questions 7 and 8.

11. Plot a graph using the following data. The data give the temperatures on a factory floor at noon. Is there any trend to the temperatures?

Temperature in °C	18	18	20	19	20	23	21	21
Date in month	1	2	3	4	5	6	7	8

Force

12. If we take 1 N to be about 100 gf, what will be the value in newtons of (a) 200 gf, (b) 1 kgf, (c) 6 kgf?

Stretching and compressing

13. Plot a load–extension graph from the following results, obtained when a mild steel specimen was pulled in a tensile testing machine:

Load in kg	0	500	1000	1500	2000	2500
Extension in mm	0	0·014	0·027	0·040	0·054	0·068

(a) What is the extension for a load of 1200 kg?
(b) What load is necessary to produce an extension of 0·020 mm?

14. Is Hooke's law obeyed in the following?

(a) Load in kg	0	200	400	600	800
Extension in mm	0	0·007	0·015	0·022	0·030
(b) Load in kN	0	10	20	30	40
Extension in mm	0	0·024	0·060	0·088	0·118

15. Explain, in your own words, what is meant by the terms elastic, brittle, and ductile.

The structure of solids

16. Explain to a fellow student, who missed the lessons, the reasons for considering crystals to offer evidence for the atomic structure of matter.

17. About how many atoms would you have to put in a line to cover a distance of 1 mm?

18. In the year 1890 Lord Rayleigh found that a drop of olive oil of volume 0·0009 cm^3, when dropped on to a water surface, spread out until it covered an area of 5500 cm^2. What is the thickness of the oil film? What does this tell you about the size of the olive oil molecule?

Compounds and mixtures

19. How would you extract salt from a solution of salt in water?

20. Why do you think water is a compound and not a mixture of hydrogen and oxygen?

Elements

21. In your own words, state what an element is. How does an element differ from a compound?

Solutions

22. Plot a graph for the following data which gives the amounts of salt needed to saturate 100 g of water at different temperatures:

Mass of salt in g	35·7	36·0	36·6	37·3	38·4	39·8
Temperature in °C	0	20	40	60	80	100

Discussion points

The following points are intended to serve as possible subjects for discussion.

Modern architecture uses new materials to produce structures which are quite different in appearance from those of earlier periods. Modern structures look quite open. How is this a product of the new materials? How have building materials changed over the years?

Background reading

Harding, D. W., and L. Griffiths, 'Materials', *Physics Topics*, Longman, 1968.

Hurst, M. M., 'Crystals', *Physics Topics*, Longman, 1969.

2. Structures

2.1 Forces

If two people push you they are applying forces to you. If they pull you they are also applying forces to you. Forces are pushes and pulls. But in order to work out the effect of these forces you need to know not only how big the forces are, but in what direction the forces are acting. If the two people pushing you are pushing in opposite directions, one pushing against your back the other against your front, then the final effect could be that you are a bit squashed. If one was pushing much harder than the other then you might be a bit squashed and also pushed backwards, or forwards. If both were pushing against your back then you would be pushed forwards. The effect depends not only on the size of the forces, but their directions.

Forces are *vector* quantities. A vector quantity needs both its size, or magnitude, and its direction specified if its effect is to be forecast. Quantities for which only the magnitude is important are called *scalar* quantities. Volume is a scalar quantity. If you take two litres of water and add three litres of water then the result is five litres. Direction has no significance when we deal with volumes.

Forces are pushes or pulls. If, however, we do not see the push or pull being applied how can we judge when a force is being applied? We look for the effects of the force. When people push or pull you, you become a bit squashed or extended or movement occurs. Forces cause changes in shape or changes in motion. An object at rest might start to move or it might, if already in motion, change its motion. Because the direction of a force is significant we can apply two opposite and equal forces to an object and end up with no motion, only extension or compression of the object. We say that in such a case there is no resultant force; no change in motion means no resultant force. If the two people pushing on you push with opposite and equal forces, perhaps one pushing your back and the other your front, then there is no change in motion and hence no resultant force. The forces are said to be in *equilibrium*.

Suppose we were to take a trolley and attach a spring balance to it; Fig. 2.1(a). When we pull on the spring balance a reading is indicated on the balance and the trolley moves. If we attach two spring balances to the trolley, and arrange them so that they pull in exactly opposite directions (Fig. 2.1(b)), then no movement occurs when the balances read the same force. The forces are in equilibrium.

16

There is another equilibrium condition which will be met later in this chapter. The two spring balances can read the same force and there be a net force of zero acting on the trolley, when the trolley is at rest or is moving with a constant velocity. Only when there is a net force on the trolley is there an acceleration.

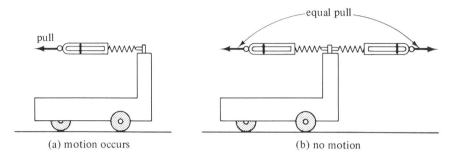

(a) motion occurs   (b) no motion

Fig. 2.1

2.2 Forces in equilibrium

We can have equilibrium with two opposite and equal forces. Thus, if we have an object which is motionless and we know there is one force acting on it, perhaps a gravitational force, then we know that there must be an opposite and equal force somewhere which is balancing out the force we know

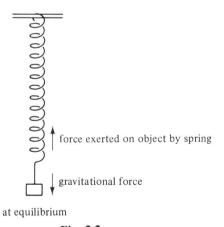

force exerted on object by spring

gravitational force

at equilibrium

Fig. 2.2

of. We cannot have a net force acting on an object if that object is motionless. For example, if we suspend an object from a spring then the spring stretches until the gravitational force acting on the object is equalled by the upward force on the object exerted by the spring; Fig. 2.2.

But suppose we have more than two forces acting at a point, what then is the condition for equilibrium? The condition is still that there be no net force acting at the point if there is no movement. Suppose we take three spring balances and hook them together; Fig. 2.3. We can exert different forces on the junction point by pulling each balance in different directions and with different forces. You might like to try this as an experiment, and see if you can find any pattern in the results when no movement occurs of the junction.

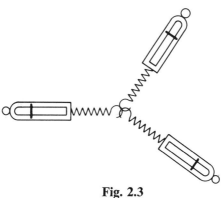

Fig. 2.3

If we draw on paper an arrow, and make the length of it represent the size of the force, e.g., 2 cm length is equivalent to 20 N or 1 cm to 10 N; and if we make the direction of the arrow the same as the direction in which the force is acting, then a pattern to the results of the equilibrium of three forces acting at a point can be found. Suppose we have the arrangement of spring balances pulling on a common junction point that results in one indicating a force of 20 N in one direction, another 29 N in a different direction, and the third 35 N in yet another direction; Fig. 2.4. To represent the 20 N force we draw an arrow 2 cm long in the direction of the force. For the 29 N force we draw an arrow 2·9 cm long, since we are taking 1 cm to represent 10 N, in the direction of that force. For the 35 N force we draw an arrow 3·5 cm long in the correct direction. These three arrows can be repositioned, and then form the three sides of a triangle. It is only when the three forces are in equilibrium that they do form a complete triangle.

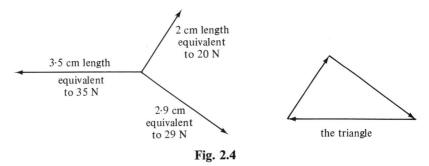

Fig. 2.4

The resulting triangle is called the *triangle of forces*. The triangle is a pattern, a relationship for three forces in equilibrium. Much of science concerns examining data and looking for patterns.

If a mass is suspended from a wire, then the forces pulling on the wire due to the gravitational force on the mass can be determined by using the triangle of forces as illustrated in Fig. 2.5. Using a scale of 1 cm to 20 N, a line of length 5 cm can be drawn to represent the gravitational force on

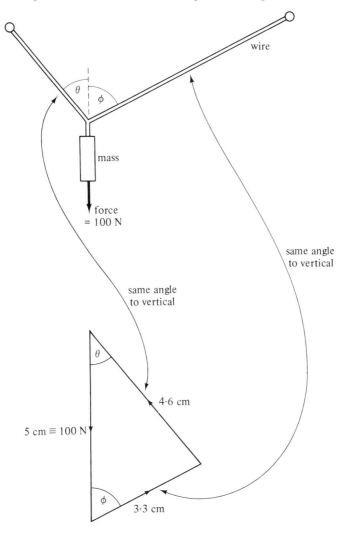

scale: 1 cm ≡ 20 N

thus forces are 3·3 × 20 = 66 N
and 4·6 × 20 = 92 N

Fig. 2.5

19

the mass. The other forces are drawn in at the correct angles, and the triangle is completed where these two lines intersect. The magnitude of the forces can be calculated from the length of the lines.

We can use this pattern to find the resultant force acting on a body when that body is subject to more than one force. If we have two forces acting on the object, with what single force can we replace those two forces and still have the same effect? Suppose the body to be in equilibrium under the action of two forces; these forces would have to be opposite and equal in size. Suppose the body to be in equilibrium under the action of three forces and we wanted to replace two of these forces by a single force. This single force would have to be opposite and equal to the third equilibrium force. So to find the resultant of two forces we have to find the force that would be needed to keep equilibrium, and then say that the resultant force of the two is opposite and equal in size. The resultant can be obtained by drawing a parallelogram, the sides representing the forces concerned, as shown in Fig. 2.6.

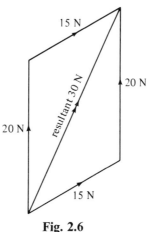

Fig. 2.6

2.3 Reaction forces

Suppose you were to stand on a trampoline. The trampoline would stretch (Fig. 2.7). The reason for it stretching is that your mass is acted on by gravity and your feet press down against the trampoline. When you stand on the ground you are exerting a force on the ground, in the same way as with the trampoline. If you stand on a bathroom scales your mass is acted on by gravity which pulls you down against the scales. If your feet did not press down on the scales you would obtain no weight reading by the scales. If you hang a mass on the end of a vertical, suspended spring then the spring stretches. The spring stretches until the downward gravitational force is balanced by the upward directed force produced by the stretching of the spring. When you stand on the trampoline it stretches and you sink down

20

until the downward directed force is just balanced by a force produced by the stretching of the trampoline. These upward directed forces are called *reaction forces*. When you stand on the ground there is an upward directed reaction force which just balances out the downward directed gravitational force acting on you. If the net force acting on you was not zero then you would accelerate and probably disappear into the ground!

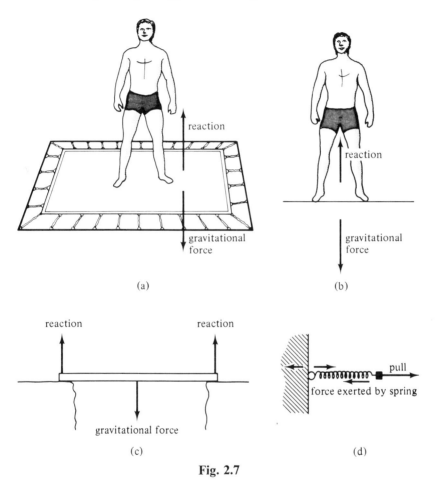

Fig. 2.7

Suppose you take a spring and anchor one end of it to the wall (Fig. 2.7) and then pull on the free end of the spring in such a way as to keep the spring horizontal. When you pull on the spring the spring stretches. It keeps on stretching until the force exerted by you is balanced by the force exerted on you by the spring. At the other end of the spring the spring is pulling on the wall. Because that end of the spring does not move, the force exerted by the spring on the wall must be balanced by the force exerted by the wall on the spring. If this did not occur, then the wall would start to move.

21

2.4 Supported beams

A simple supported beam is a see-saw, a uniform beam resting across a centrally placed pivot. When equal loads are placed at the two ends of this centrally supported beam then equilibrium occurs. If, however, the loads are not equal or are not placed the same distances from the central pivot then the beam tends to rotate about the central pivot, Fig. 2.8. What is the

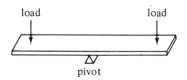

Fig. 2.8

pattern covering equilibrium for a see-saw? Experiments can be done, placing different loads at different distances from the pivot, and noting when equilibrium occurs. Typical results for a laboratory experiment using equal coins placed on a centrally pivoted rule are:

Number of coins on left side	Distance on left from pivot, in cm	Number of coins on right side	Distance on right from pivot, in cm
1	20	1	20
2	20	2	20
3	20	3	20
1	10	1	10
2	10	2	10
3	10	3	10

A load at some distance on the left-hand side is balanced by the same load at the same distance on the other side. Putting the same load at a different distance results in the beam going out of equilibrium. For equilibrium we have:

Number of coins on left side	Distance on left from pivot, in cm	Number of coins on right side	Distance on right from pivot, in cm
1	20	2	10
1	20	4	5
2	20	4	10
2	20	8	5
2	10	1	20
2	10	4	5

What is the pattern in these results? If you multiply the number of coins on the left-hand side by the distance they are from the pivot, the result is equal to the product of the number of coins on the right-hand side multiplied by the distance they are from the pivot, when equilibrium occurs. The number of the coins is a measure of the force acting on the beam at the point concerned. Hence the product of the force and its distance from the pivot on the left-hand side is equal to the product of the force and its distance from the pivot on the right-hand side. The force on the left-hand side is endeavouring to produce an anticlockwise rotation of the beam about the pivot; the force on the right-hand side is endeavouring to produce a clockwise rotation about the pivot. The product of the force and the perpendicular distance from the line, along which it is acting, to the pivot is called the *moment* of the force. Thus for equilibrium we must have the clockwise moment about the pivot being balanced by the anticlockwise moment.

What if the pivot is not central? Well, in some of the above the pivot was not central between the loads, but the clockwise moment still equals the anticlockwise moment for equilibrium.

2.5 Centre of mass

If I carefully place a ruler horizontally across my outstretched finger I can balance the rule. It looks rather like the see-saw without any loads being applied to either side of the pivot, my finger. But there is a load—the ruler itself; it has mass and so there is a gravitational force acting on the ruler. The only way we can really explain the anticlockwise and clockwise moments being equal for this situation is to think of the ruler being made up of a very large number of small pieces of matter. There is a small piece 10 cm on the left-hand side of the pivot; there is an exactly corresponding piece 10 cm away on the right-hand side. This assumes a uniform ruler. At equilibrium, for every piece we have on the left-hand side there is a corresponding piece an equal distance away on the right-hand side, Fig. 2.9.

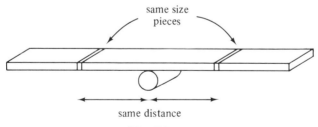

same size
pieces

same distance

Fig. 2.9

Suppose the ruler had a mass of 10 g. Now, suppose that, instead of balancing the ruler on my finger, I balance a very light strip of, say, expanded polystyrene. The mass of this strip is very small in comparison with 10 g. The strip balances in the same way as the ruler. Now, if I add sufficient mass to this strip to bring its total mass up to 10 g there is only one place I can put a single block of mass and still have the strip in equilibrium. That place is directly over the pivot. Our 10 g ruler behaves as though all its mass was located at just one point, a point directly over the pivot point. This point on the ruler is called its *centre of mass* (sometimes also referred to as the centroid).

Suppose you were to take a non-regular object. If you suspend it so that it can freely rotate, then it always moves until the centre of mass lies along a vertical line through the point of suspension; Fig. 2.10. When this occurs there is no unbalanced moment, there is equilibrium. This gives only the line along which the centre of mass lies. If you suspend the object about other points then you can obtain a number of lines along which the centre of mass must lie. Where these lines intersect must be the centre of mass.

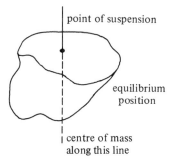

point of suspension

equilibrium position

centre of mass along this line

Fig. 2.10

The centre of mass of a uniformly dense sphere is at the centre of the sphere. If we put a sphere on a convex surface then we can balance it at some point, but the slightest disturbance causes the sphere to roll off; Fig. 2.11. This form of initial equilibrium is called *unstable*, because the slightest touch causes the equilibrium to vanish. If we put the ball on a concave surface then a disturbance causes the ball to roll initially but soon return to its original equilibrium position. Such a position is called *stable*. If we put the ball on a horizontal surface then a push causes the ball to move but, generally, it will come to rest in another equilibrium position. Such a position is called *neutral* equilibrium. What distinguishes these three forms of equilibrium? In the

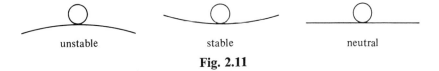

unstable   stable   neutral

Fig. 2.11

unstable form the movement allows the centre of mass to fall; in the stable form any movement causes the centre of mass to rise; in the neutral case there is no change in the height of the centre of mass. This is the pattern of results that is found whatever the object is. In the unstable position the force of gravity on the centre of mass tends to pull it away from its initial position; in the stable position the gravitational force pulls the object back to its initial position; in the neutral case the force does not pull the object either away or back to its initial position.

If a cube is tilted, the cube is stable until the tilt moves the centre of mass beyond the vertical line passing through the pivot, the corner of the cube about which it is tilted; Fig. 2.12(a). Beyond that point the cube will fall over. If the cube is uniform the centre of mass is in the centre. However, if we consider a car: for the car to be in stable equilibrium when tilted, e.g., when cornering, the centre of mass of the car must not move beyond the vertical line passing through the pivot, i.e., the pair of wheels on that side; Fig. 2.12(b). Thus for the safest cornering, i.e., the maximum tilt angle, the centre of mass should be as low as possible.

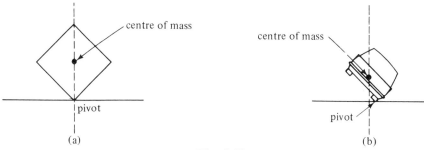

Fig. 2.12

2.6 A simple bridge

A simple form of bridge is a plank across a gap, each end of the plank resting on the bank; Fig. 2.13. We will assume that the plank is in equilibrium when a man is standing at the centre, and the arrows in Fig. 2.13 indicate the direction of the forces. To begin with we will neglect the weight of the plank itself, and consider only the weight of the man as being responsible

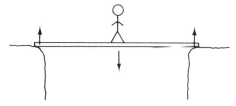

Fig. 2.13

for a downward force on the plank. Where the plank rests on the bank we must have upward directed forces exerted by the ground on the plank. Because the plank is in equilibrium, these upward directed forces must be equal in size to the downward directed force due to the gravitational force acting on the man. Suppose this force on the man is 600 N. Then we must have:

sum of the upward forces acting on the plank = 600 N

25

As the man is exactly half-way between the points where these upward forces act we might guess that the two upward forces are equal in size and so, therefore, that they are each equal to 300 N.

There is another condition which is true if an object is in equilibrium. Not only must the vector sum, i.e., the sum taking into account the directions of the forces, be zero, but the sum of the moments of all the forces considered relative to any point must be zero. We can put this another way: no point behaves as a pivot about which rotation occurs. If there was rotation we would not consider there to be equilibrium.

If we consider the clockwise moments of the forces about any point then they must be equal to the anticlockwise moments. Suppose we take the point A in Fig. 2.14, where one end of the bridge rests on the bank, as a possible pivot point. If the bridge is of length L, then the man is a distance

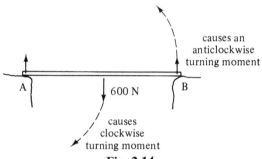

Fig. 2.14

$\frac{1}{2}L$ from the bank. We have put him half-way across the bridge. If the bridge was of length 4 m then the man would be $\frac{1}{2} \times 4 = 2$ m from the bank. Hence the turning moment of the force due to the man, about the bank at A, is $600 \times \frac{1}{2}L$ or, in the case of the 4 m bridge, $600 \times 2 = 1200$ Nm. The turning moment of the force at the far end of the bridge, B, is $F \times L$, or in the case of the 4 m bridge $F \times 4$. There is no other force producing a moment and so we must have

$$600 \times \tfrac{1}{2}L = F \times L \quad \text{or} \quad 1200 = F \times 4$$

Hence F, the force exerted at B by the bank on the bridge, must be 300 N.

If we want to take into account the weight of the bridge then we consider the weight to be acting at the centre of mass i.e., the centre of the bridge, and solve the problem with the addition of this force. Suppose the weight were 40 N. Then we must have:

$$\text{sum of upward forces} = 600 + 40$$

and when we take moments about the end A:

$$600 \times \tfrac{1}{2}L + 40 \times \tfrac{1}{2}L = F \times L$$

Hence we have F equal to 320 N. The force at each end of the bridge is the same.

2.7 Materials for structures

A wall relies for its strength on compressive forces; Fig. 2.15. Each brick presses down on the brick beneath it and exerts a force on it, which results in compression of the brick. The mortar between the bricks is to keep the bricks in place. The wall, however, is only strong in compression. An upward pull will separate the bricks, and a sideways push can dislodge the mortar. Brick building depends on the weight of the building, pushing down on the bricks, to keep the structure erect.

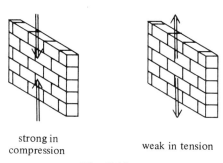

strong in
compression

weak in tension

Fig. 2.15

Wood is stronger in tension than in compression, and so to make the most use of the strength of wood it should be used in tension rather than compression. The compressive strength of concrete is some five times greater than its tensile strength, and thus, it is best used in situations where the concrete is in compression rather than in tension. The use of steel reinforcing bars in concrete gives a composite which has better strength in tension than the concrete alone.

Hence, if we consider our simple bridge, i.e., a plank resting at each end on the banks of a river, then for the buttresses to support the ends of the plank we need a material which is strong in compression, because the forces exerted by the plank on the banks are such as to compress the bank. Buttresses made of brick or concrete might thus be suitable. For the plank we tend to think in the simplest case of wood. A man standing on the bridge

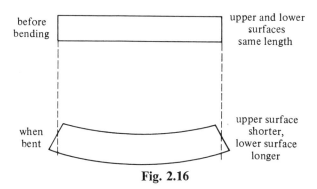

before
bending

upper and lower
surfaces
same length

when
bent

upper surface
shorter,
lower surface
longer

Fig. 2.16

will be pushing down on the bridge and causing the lower surface of the bridge to extend and the upper surface to compress; Fig. 2.16. The upper surface of the plank is thus in compression, the lower in tension. If we wanted to make the 'plank' out of concrete and reinforce the concrete with steel bars, then the steel bars should be put in the lower part of the concrete beam, where the concrete is put into tension. Designing a structure means more than just calculating forces, the correct materials have to be found to withstand the forces.

Problems

Forces

1. In your own words explain what is meant by the scientific term 'force'.
2. Which of the following would you consider to be vector, and which scalar, quantities: force, mass, volume, temperature?
3. An object when pushed acquires speed; its motion changes. When we stop pushing the object may continue in motion for a while, but eventually comes to rest. Something is changing its motion when we stop pushing. What is the source of this force?

Forces in equilibrium

4. If I pull on a block with a force of 30 N, what force must be applied, and what must be its direction, to keep the block from moving?
5. If I push against a table and perhaps push with a force of 20 N, and the table does not move, how is it possible to explain that the action of the force does not give rise to motion?
6. Determine the force that has to be applied to balance out the effects of:
   (a) 30 N and 40 N at right-angles,
   (b) 30 N and 40 N at 45° to each other,
   (c) 30 N and 40 N in direct opposition to each other.
   In each case state the direction of the force, as well as its size.
7. A mass of 5 kg is supported by two wires inclined at angles of 60° and 30° to the vertical. Determine the tension in the wires.

Reaction forces

8. Estimate the reaction force when you stand on a level floor. Guess the data you need.

Supported beams

9. A see-saw is pivoted at its centre. At one end, 1 m from the pivot, a boy with a mass of 30 kg sits. Where should a girl of mass 25 kg sit if the see-saw is to balance, i.e., be in equilibrium?

10. Complete the following table for a centrally pivoted see-saw:

Left-hand side	*Right-hand side*
(a) 30 kg 120 cm from pivot	X kg 100 cm from pivot
(b) 40 kg 150 cm from pivot	50 kg X cm from pivot
(c) X kg 100 cm from pivot	20 kg 80 cm from pivot
(d) 30 kg X cm from pivot	40 kg 30 cm from pivot
(e) 300 N force 100 cm from pivot	X N force 90 cm from pivot

Centre of mass

11. At what point should a rule, 50 cm long and 2 cm wide, balance?

12. How could you find, experimentally, the centre of mass of a tapered shaft?

13. To what angle should you be able to tilt, about one edge, a uniform cube before it topples?

14. The front wheels of a bus are 2 m apart; the wheels at the rear of the bus are also 2 m apart. When the vehicle is tilted about the wheels on one side, toppling starts to occur when the axles are inclined at 30° to the horizontal. What is the vertical height of the centre of mass above the road surface? Why are there restrictions on the number of passengers allowed upstairs on a double-decker bus?

A simple bridge

15. A 3 m long plank is to be supported by two vertical chains attached at each end. If the plank has a weight of 100 N, what will be the tension in the chains?

16. A bridge spans a gap of 15 m and has a weight of 200 000 N. What are the reactions at the two buttresses on which the bridge is supported at each end? How are the reactions changed when a lorry with a weight of 50 000 N is 3 m from one of the buttresses? With just one such lorry on the bridge what will be its position for the maximum reaction at any one buttress? What will be the value of this reaction?

17. Figure 2.17 shows a simplified diagram of the human forearm being used to lift a load. If the lower end of the biceps muscle is attached 5 cm

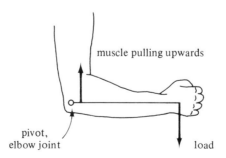

Fig. 2.17

from the elbow joint, and a load of 20 N is lifted by the hand, a distance of 30 cm from the elbow joint, what will be the force that the muscle needs to exert? What will be the reaction at the elbow joint?

Discussion points

The suspension bridge across the river Severn was opened to the public in 1966. Look at maps for that area and consider how the bridge shortened the distance by road between Bristol and Cardiff. What effect do you think this had on industry in South Wales?

Background reading

Rolt, L. T. C., *Isambard Kingdom Brunel*, Penguin, 1970.
  Chapter 4 of this book gives some of the background to the building of the suspension bridge at Clifton, Bristol.

3. Forces and motion

3.1 Describing motion

The terms speed and acceleration are used in everyday language; in science they have been given very specific meanings which, in general, reflect the meanings given to them in everyday language. Thus *speed* is defined as the rate of covering distance.

$$\text{average speed} = \frac{\text{distance travelled}}{\text{time taken}}$$

Thus if 50 kilometres are covered in an hour then the average speed is 50 kilometres per hour, i.e., 50 km/h. The speed is described as being the 'average' because there can be variations of speed within the time interval, and we cannot say from the data that the speed was constant for the entire time. Thus, for the 50 km/h the speed could have been 60 km/h for perhaps 5 minutes and 40 km/h for 5 minutes. The important thing is that the total distance covered divided by the time gives the overall performance for the hour. If we want the speed at some instant then we have to consider what must be a very small time interval, in fact vanishingly small, and the distance covered in that time.

Uniform speed is attained when equal distances are covered in equal intervals of time, however small the time intervals considered. Thus, a uniform speed of 50 km/h means that if we examine 5 minutes, or 1 minute, or 1 second, of the motion we will find that the speed is still 50 km/h. Distance is being covered at the rate of 50 km every hour.

The term velocity is not, in scientific language, the same as speed. If we have a speed of 50 km/h then this means that 50 km are covered in an hour. The information does not enable you to say where, with reference to a starting point, you might find the moving object at the end of an hour. It could be 50 km away, perhaps due north of the starting point, or it could be back at the starting point having travelled in a circular path. Just the knowledge that the speed was 50 km/h does not enable you to determine its displacement from a starting point. If, however, you were told that the velocity was 50 km/h then the object must be 50 km away after an hour. *Velocity* is defined as the distance travelled in a straight line divided by the time taken.

$$\text{average velocity} = \frac{\text{distance travelled in a straight line}}{\text{time taken}}$$

Acceleration is defined as the velocity change divided by the time taken for the change.

$$\text{average acceleration} = \frac{\text{velocity change}}{\text{time taken}}$$

Thus if the velocity changes from 30 to 35 km/h in a time of 1 minute then the acceleration is $35 - 30 = 5$ km/h per minute. If the velocity changed from 5 to 7 m per second in 1 second then the acceleration would be $7 - 5 = 2$ m per second per second. The units are generally written as metres/second² (m/s²).

Units

The units of speed are obtained by dividing the units of distance by those of time.

$$\frac{\text{distance unit}}{\text{time unit}} = \frac{\text{metre}}{\text{second}}$$

The u it can thus be metre/second. The / sign or the word 'per' means that the first unit before the sign is divided by the unit after the sign. The units of velocity are the same as those of speed.

The units of acceleration are obtained by dividing the units of velocity by those of time.

$$\frac{\text{velocity unit}}{\text{time unit}} = \frac{\text{metre/second}}{\text{second}}$$

We can rearrange these units to give:

$$\frac{\text{metre}}{\text{second} \times \text{second}} = \frac{\text{metre}}{\text{second}^2} = \text{m/s}^2$$

3.2 Graphically describing motion

The quantities that are measured in many cases are distances and times. It could be the record of a truck moving along a track or a piston moving in a cylinder. The following data could refer to the truck:

Distance moved, in metres	0	100	200	300	400	500
Time taken, in seconds (s)	0	25	45	60	75	90

The truck takes 25 s to cover the first 100 m; it takes 45 s to cover the first 200 m. You might think of the data being collected by men standing at the zero, 100 m, 200 m, 300 m, 400 m, and 500 m points. When the man at the zero point gives the signal the truck starts, and each of the other men starts a stopwatch. When the truck reaches a man he stops his watch and notes the time.

We can describe the motion of the truck by tabulating the data, or by using the data to produce a graph. Figure 3.1 shows the graph constructed from the above data. Figure 3.1 also shows the relationship between the two sets of data by a mapping.

In the first 25 s the truck covers 100 m; the next 100 m, however, only take a further 20 s. The truck is covering 100 m in a smaller time—it is moving faster—it has a higher average speed for the second 100 m distance.

$$\text{For the first 100 m, average speed} = \frac{100}{25} = 4 \text{ m/s}$$

$$\text{For the second 100 m, average speed} = \frac{100}{20} = 5 \text{ m/s}$$

In Fig. 3.2, the slope of the graph has increased. We define the slope of the graph (the word gradient or even steepness may be used) as being the

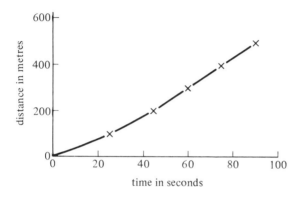

(a)

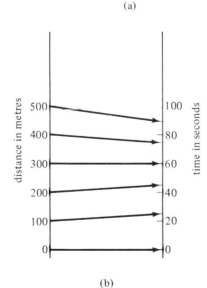

(b)

Fig. 3.1

33

change in the quantity given by the graphical vertical axis, divided by the change in the horizontal axis quantity corresponding to the vertical change. Figure 3.2 shows this. But this quantity 'slope' is nothing more than the distance travelled divided by the time taken, when the graph is of distance against time. The slope is thus the speed. The higher the speed, the greater the slope.

Between 200 and 300 m, between 300 and 400 m, between 400 and 500 m, the same time is taken to cover the same distance. This means that the speed is the same for each of these distances. On the graph, in Fig. 3.1, this shows as a line with a constant slope.

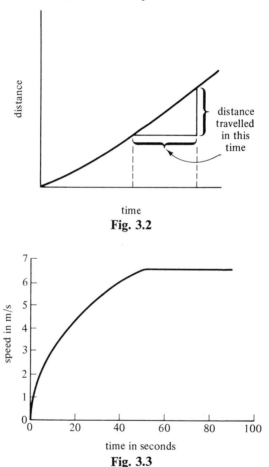

Fig. 3.2

Fig. 3.3

We could also describe the motion of the truck by plotting a graph of velocity, i.e., the slopes at different points on the distance–time graph, against time. Where the velocity is constant the graph line is parallel to the time axis. Where the velocity is changing the slope of the graph changes. The slope of this graph is the acceleration, and so a constant acceleration is indicated by a constant slope, i.e., a straight line. Figure 3.3 shows the graph for the truck.

3.3 Equations describing motion

The average velocity is the distance travelled in a straight line divided by the time taken. If we represent these quantities by symbols, d for distance, t for time and $\bar{v}$ for average velocity, then we have:

$$\bar{v} = \frac{d}{t}$$

If we look at a graph of velocity against time, Fig. 3.4, and only consider motion with uniform acceleration, then the average velocity for an object accelerating from an initial velocity v_0 to velocity v_1 is half-way between those two values. This half-way value is

$$\bar{v} = \frac{v_0 + v_1}{2}$$

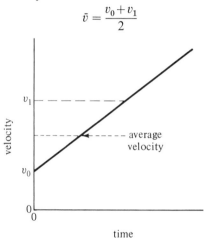

Fig. 3.4

Thus, if the initial velocity was 3 m/s and the final velocity was 7 m/s then the average velocity would be $(3+7)$ divided by 2, i.e., 5 m/s.

If the object accelerates from 3 to 7 m/s in 2 s then the distance covered will be given by

$$\bar{v} = 5 = \frac{d}{t} = \frac{d}{2}$$

Hence

$$d = 10 \text{ m}$$

Acceleration is given by the velocity change divided by the time taken. This is the slope of the velocity–time graph. If we write a to represent the acceleration, then

$$a = \frac{v_1 - v_0}{t}$$

t is the time interval in which the velocity changes from v_0 to v_1. Thus, in the above example, where the velocity changes from 3 to 7 m/s in 2 s we must have an average acceleration of

$$a = \frac{7-3}{2}$$

$$a = 2 \text{ m/s}^2$$

This equation for acceleration can be rearranged to give the form most usually seen in books.

Multiplying both sides of the equation by t gives

$$a \times t = \frac{v_1 - v_0}{t} \times t$$

$$at = v_1 - v_0$$

Adding v_0 to both sides gives

$$v_0 + at = v_1$$

Suppose we have a truck accelerating, uniformly, at 3 m/s² from an initial velocity of 2 m/s, its velocity after $\frac{1}{2}$ s at this acceleration is given by

$$v_0 + at = v_1$$
$$2 + 3 \times \tfrac{1}{2} = v_1$$

Hence v_1 is $3\frac{1}{2}$ m/s, the velocity after $\frac{1}{2}$ s.

The equation, $v_1 = v_0 + at$, is the equation which tells how the velocity of a uniformly accelerating object changes with time. It is the equation of the line in the velocity–time graph in Fig. 3.4. The equation is of the form $y = c + mx$, the equation of a straight line. The slope m is the acceleration, y is the velocity corresponding to the time t, which is represented by x. The intercept c is the initial velocity v_0.

3.4 Reaction time

Suppose you are driving a car and suddenly the brake lights of the car in front of you flash on. Your foot moves on to the brake pedal. But your foot does not move immediately you see the brake lights; you need time to react. This reaction time is typically of the order of one-half of a full second. The value depends on you and on your condition: half asleep, wide awake, slowed down by alcohol. If you were travelling at 30 km/h and your reaction time was 0·7 s then you would travel a distance of about $5\frac{1}{2}$ m before your foot hits the brake pedal.

30 km/h is about 8 m/s and thus

$$v = 8 = \frac{d}{t} = \frac{d}{0·7}$$

36

and so
$$d = 5 \cdot 6 \text{ m}$$

If you were travelling at 60 km/h the distance travelled before you begin to brake would be about 11 m. This is about two car lengths. At 120 km/h the distance has become about 22 m, about four car lengths.

These distances are only the distance covered while your foot moves to apply the brakes, the car still has to slow down and this takes yet more time. Suppose the application of the brakes caused the car to decelerate at 6 m/s². The term *deceleration* is often used to mean a negative acceleration, a velocity change which in a time interval means a reduction rather than an increase of velocity. The acceleration is, thus, -6 m/s².

$$v_0 + at = v_1$$

For an initial velocity of 16 m/s, i.e., about 60 km/h, and a final velocity of zero (the car stopped) we have

$$16 - 6 \times t = 0$$

Adding $6t$ to both sides of the equation gives

$$16 = 6t$$

The time taken to come to rest is thus $2\frac{2}{3}$ s. We can calculate how far the car would travel in this time. The average velocity is half of 16, i.e., 8 m/s and so the distance is $21\frac{1}{3}$ m. The total distance travelled from seeing the brake lights come on to the car coming to rest is thus about 32 m. I leave you to work out the total stopping distance for higher velocities.

3.5 Forces and motion

Suppose we roll a ball down one side of a U-shaped track, Fig. 3.5, how far up the other side of the track will the ball roll? Well, if you try the experiment you will find that the ball rolls up the other side of the U almost as far as the

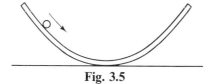

Fig. 3.5

height from which it started. Now it does not matter what the shape of the U is. Each of the U's limbs can be at different angles to the horizontal, the ball still rolls up the other side of the U to the same *height* as it started from. But what happens if we make one of the limbs of the U horizontal? Presumably the ball should come down the U limb and then run out on to the horizontal limb and keep on rolling until it comes back up to the same height as it started from; which it cannot do. The ball should therefore, theoretically, go on rolling for ever. If it goes on rolling for ever then the velocity of the ball might be expected to be unchanging.

You may feel that the above is unrealistic; balls set in motion do not go on rolling for ever. They slow down and, eventually, come to rest. If they roll over a rough surface they slow down more rapidly than if they roll over a smooth surface. Suppose we had a perfectly smooth surface then, perhaps, the ball would go on rolling for ever. Instead of 'perfectly smooth' it is clearer to talk of a *frictionless* motion. A ball slows down because of *friction*. In the absence of friction, it seems that the ball would go on rolling for ever. This is known as *Newton's first law of motion: an object remains at rest or moves with a uniform velocity in the absence of a force*. Friction provides the force which slows down rolling balls.

When the velocity of an object changes there must be a force acting and causing the change. We detect this as an acceleration. Whenever there is an acceleration a force must be acting.

Figure 3.6 shows what happens when an object moves under almost frictionless conditions. The object shown in the photograph is similar to a hovercraft in principle; it floats on a cushion of gas. The photographs show a number of images of the object at different instances, the time between any successive pair of images being the same. With no force, Fig. 3.6(a), the object just continues in motion with a uniform velocity. With a force acting, Fig. 3.6(b), the object accelerates. You can easily tell from the photograph

(a)

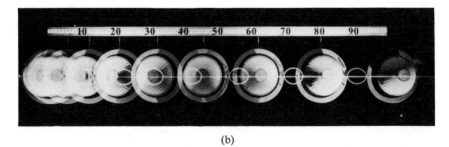

(b)

Fig. 3.6 (a) and (b); in (b) the flash photographs show the puck being pulled to the right (from *PSSC Physics*, 2nd edn, courtesy D. C. Heath and Company, Lexington, Ma.)

38

that the object is accelerating—the distances between successive images are increasing. Only when the velocity is constant will the distances between successive images remain constant, i.e., equal distances are covered in equal intervals of time.

How is the acceleration of an object related to the force exerted on it? To determine this, experimentally, we need to find some way of specifying the forces. A simple way of doing this is to use the extension of a rubber band or a spring, something which gives a measurable extension when acted on by forces. Suppose we use a rubber band to apply the force and suppose we apply the force to a trolley, Fig. 3.7, then we suppose that a constant force is applied when the extension of the rubber band remains constant. When we want to apply double the force then we use two identical rubber bands, each stretched by the same amount as the band used for the single force. For triple the force we use three rubber bands, all stretched the same amount.

The accelerations of the trolleys can be determined by taking multiflash photographs, like those shown in Fig. 3.6, or by the use of ticker tape and a vibrator (see questions 22–24 at the end of this chapter). The tape, a long strip of paper, is attached at one end to the trolley and passes under a vibrator which makes marks on the paper at regular intervals of time. When the trolley moves it pulls the tape under the vibrator. The length of the tape pulled under the vibrator gives a measure of the distance the trolley has moved, the number of marks on the paper indicates how much time has elapsed; Fig. 3.7.

The results of such experiments can be summarized as

Force	Acceleration
one rubber band	a
two rubber bands	$2a$
three rubber bands	$3a$

If one rubber band gave an acceleration of 2 m/s², then two rubber bands gave 4 m/s², three rubber bands 6 m/s². The acceleration is directly proportional to the force.

There is another factor. If we pull two trolleys instead of just one then we have, with one rubber band exerting the force, just half the acceleration obtained with the single trolley. Doubling the number of trolleys halves the acceleration. What we really have done is double something we call *mass*. Double the mass means half the acceleration.

The relationship of force and mass with acceleration can be represented by the equation

$$F = ma$$

Put your finger over m and you have $F \propto a$; put it over F and you have constant $= ma$ or

$$a \propto \frac{1}{m}$$

39

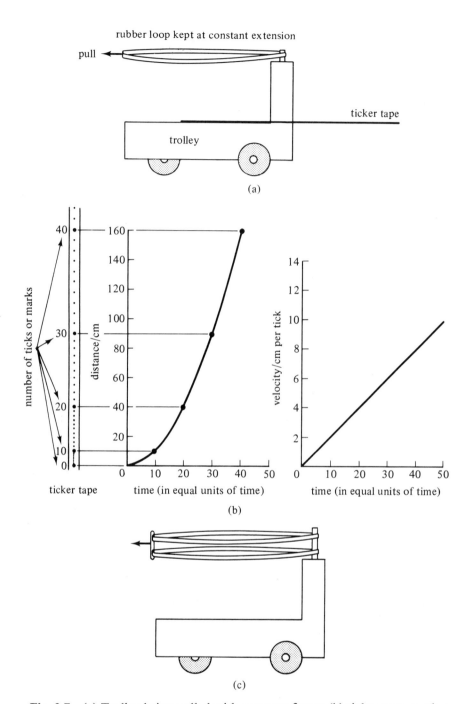

Fig. 3.7 (a) Trolley being pulled with constant force; (b) ticker tape results; (c) trolley being pulled with double the force in (a) (from *Patterns in Physics*, W. Bolton, McGraw-Hill, 1974)

Thus, acceleration is *inversely proportional* to mass. If the acceleration a has units of m/s² and the mass is measured in kilogrammes, then the unit of force is defined as the newton.

If we have a force of 4 N acting on a mass of 2 kg, then the acceleration is given by

$$F = 4 = ma = 2a$$

Hence

$$a = 2 \text{ m/s}^2$$

If we double the mass to 4 kg for the same force then

$$F = 4 = 4a$$

Hence

$$a = 1 \text{ m/s}^2$$

Doubling the mass has halved the acceleration for the same force.

What is the thing we call mass? If we increase the mass for the same force we reduce the acceleration. The bigger the mass the smaller is the acceleration. If you apply equal pushes to two different objects then the object with the smallest mass moves away the quicker; it has the bigger acceleration. Mass represents something we can call *inertia*. Mass represents the ease with which an object is able to accelerate.

The standard unit of mass is the kilogramme and is given by a standard block of material. The international standard is kept in Paris. Copies of this standard are kept in many countries, their copies being compared with the Paris standard.

3.6 Free fall

When a ball falls freely, of what form is the motion? Figure 3.8(a) shows a multiflash photograph of a freely falling ball. Figures 3.8(b) and (c) show the distance–time and velocity–time graphs plotted from the photograph. The distance–time graph is not a straight line—the motion, therefore, cannot be one of constant velocity as this needs a straight-line graph. The velocity–time graph is, however, within the limits of experimental error, a straight-line graph passing through the zero velocity, zero time point. A constant slope means a constant acceleration. A freely falling object falls with a constant acceleration. The acceleration is about 10 m/s².

All objects allowed to fall freely at any one spot on the Earth have the same acceleration, when the fall is in a vacuum. The vacuum is necessary to eliminate frictional effects arising because of the presence of air. In air, for a free fall over a short distance, the acceleration will be about 10 m/s² for the fall of objects with a reasonably high density, e.g., objects like ball bearings but not objects like feathers. In a vacuum, however, a feather falls with the same acceleration as a ball bearing.

But for an acceleration to occur there must be a force. We ascribe the force, in this case, to gravitation. A force of attraction is considered to act

(a)

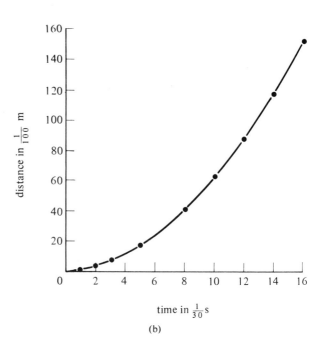

(b)

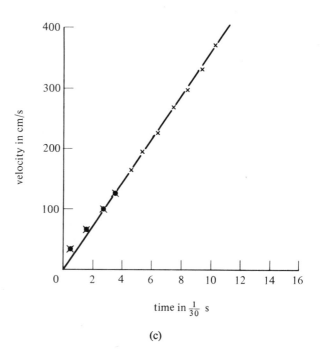

(c)

42

between any pair of objects, whether it be the force of attraction between the Sun and the Earth which is responsible for the Earth remaining in orbit about the Sun, or the force of attraction between the Earth and a stone which results in the stone falling towards the Earth when dropped.

Because this force always acts on an object we must balance out this force if we do not want an object to fall. When objects are at rest, perhaps on a table, then the gravitational force is balanced by an opposite and equal force. An object at rest on the pan of a spring balance has the gravitational force balanced by the force exerted by the spring.

If we assume Newton's laws to apply for gravitational forces acting on objects, then, if we write g to represent the acceleration due to gravity we have

$$\text{gravitational force } F = mg$$

where m is the mass of the falling object.

An object of mass 1 kg falling with an acceleration of 10 m/s^2, therefore, must be acted on by a force of 10 N. An object of mass 2 kg falls with the same acceleration, 10 m/s^2, and so must be acted on by a force of 20 N.

As has already been mentioned in chapter 1, it is often convenient to refer to forces in terms of the force that acts due to gravitation. Thus a 2 kgf is the force due to gravity which acts on a 2 kg mass, i.e., 20 N.

3.7 Energy

Suppose I lift a book from the floor to a shelf; suppose an engine runs and propels a car along a road; suppose I switch on the electricity and an electric motor runs and operates a hoist lifting a load; suppose more coal is shovelled into a furnace used to provide steam to run a turbine; suppose ... well you can no doubt think of many more instances of events involving what we call the *transfer of energy*. When I lift the book from the floor I use energy. I could use an electric motor to lift the book (Fig. 3.9) and use electric energy, or perhaps use a petrol-driven motor to do the same thing, or even use a small steam engine in which coal or some other fuel is burnt. In all the cases we talk of an energy transfer. The energy can come from the food I eat, the electricity supply, the petrol, or the coal, or oil.

What is this thing called energy? Well, we can tell when energy is being transferred to an object—it moves or it gets hot. The book, when taking energy from me, moves to a higher level: the shelf instead of the floor. This energy transfer is called *work*. The energy transfer involved in things getting hotter is called *heat*.

Fig. 3.8 (a) Strobe photograph of a falling billiard ball—the scale is in centimetres, and the light flashed every 1/30 s (from *PSSC Physics*, 2nd edn, courtesy D. C. Heath and Company, Lexington, Ma.); (b) distance–time graph (from *Patterns in Physics*, W. Bolton, McGraw-Hill, 1974); (c) velocity time graph

When I lift the book from the floor to a shelf, I am pulling the book up against the force of gravity which acts on the book. The electric motor operating a hoist lifting a load is lifting the load up against the force of gravity. Moving things against a force needs energy. In the case of a petrol-driven motor operating a hoist, I could say that the amount of petrol used is a measure of the amount of energy expended. If I lift a load vertically through 2 m I need twice the amount of fuel used for lifting the same load vertically through 1 m. Lifting the same load through 3 m takes three times the fuel. The amount of fuel used depends on the vertical distance through which the load is lifted. If I lift two of the same objects through 1 m, then twice as much fuel is necessary as when I lift just one of the objects. If the mass of the object lifted is twice as much then twice as much fuel is necessary.

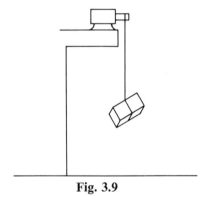

Fig. 3.9

To sum up: the amount of fuel needed depends on the vertical distance through which a load is lifted and the mass of the object lifted. But the gravitational force acting on the object depends on its mass. Thus the fuel expended depends on the force being overcome, and the distance through which the object is moved against the force. This is summarized in an equation as

$$\text{energy transfer} = \text{force} \times \text{distance}$$

This energy transfer is called work. The distance is the distance along the line of action of the force. For an object being lifted this is a vertical distance.

Work, an energy transfer, occurs when we pull on an object attached to the end of a spring; Fig. 3.10. We pull against the force exerted by the spring, and so, when we pull the object through a distance, work occurs.

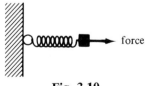

Fig. 3.10

If the force is measured in newtons and the distance in metres then the energy transferred, the work, is measured in newton metres. This unit is given a special name, a joule (J). So if we pull on an object attached to one end of a spring balance and, while we pull the object over a distance of 1/10 of a metre, along the direction in which the force acts, the balance reads 50 N, then the energy transfer is $50 \times 1/10 = 5$ J.

3.8 Conservation of energy

If I lift a book from the floor to a shelf I use energy. We can calculate a quantity called work, determined by the product of the force and distance, and call this energy transfer. But transfer to what? Why use the term transfer? It implies that the energy supplied by me in lifting the book is going somewhere else. It implies that it is not being used up, but purely given to something else. When the book is on the shelf is it any different from when it was on the floor, before I used energy to lift it? Well, when it was on the floor it had no where to fall; it can fall from the shelf back down to the floor. As it falls it will accelerate and so hit the floor with a thud—it will have a velocity on impact. Suppose the book were to fall on to the pan of a spring balance, the spring would change length; work would occur. We consider that when the book is lifted on to the shelf, energy is transferred to the book. Thus, when the book is on the shelf it has energy by virtue of its position. Such energy, position energy, is called *potential energy*. When the book falls off the shelf it loses its potential energy and, as it increases its velocity, gains movement energy. This movement energy is called *kinetic energy*. When the book hits the floor, or the pan of the balance, it stops moving and so gives up its kinetic energy. This energy is given to some other item and appears possibly in yet another form. The floor, and the book, become warmer as a result of the impact. If you hit an object repeatedly with a hammer it becomes hot. This is just like the book hitting the floor. A rise in temperature occurs, the energy is transformed to heat; Fig. 3.11.

Whatever we do all that seems to happen is that energy is transferred from object to object and from one form to another. We believe that energy is never lost, never destroyed, but always conserved. This is called the principle of the conservation of energy.

If I transfer energy by work to a book, say 5 J, then the position energy of the book will change by 5 J. A book sitting on the shelf with 5 J of potential energy falls back down to the place it started from. The 5 J of potential energy is converted into 5 J of kinetic energy. On impact this kinetic energy is converted into heat energy. There is then 5 J of heat energy.

Figure 3.11(b) shows the sequence of energy transformations for the production of electricity from falling water, i.e., hydroelectricity. Water falls from a reservoir and thus converts potential energy into kinetic energy. When the falling water hits the blades of a turbine the kinetic energy is converted into rotational energy of the turbine. The rotating turbine drives an electric generator and produces electricity. The energy is thus transformed into electrical energy. The electricity can then be fed via cables to factories, offices, houses, etc., where it can be converted into many forms. Perhaps it will drive a motor to operate a hoist, perhaps it will heat a room from an electric fire.

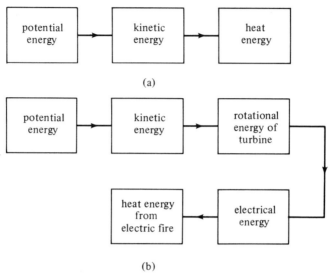

(a)

(b)

Fig. 3.11 (a) The energy transformations for a falling book; (b) the energy transformations involved with hydroelectricity

3.9 Power

The rate at which energy is transformed from one form to another is called *power*. If I lift a book up slowly and transfer 5 J of energy in 5 s, then the energy is transferred at the rate of 1 J every second. If I lift the book up quickly and take just 1 s to transfer 5 J of energy, then the rate is 5 J per second. In the first case the power was 1 J/s, in the second case 5 J/s. A power of 1 J/s is called a watt (W). The powers are thus 1 W and 5 W.

When an electric light bulb, which is marked 100 W, is connected to a mains supply of 240 volts (V), then 100 J of electrical energy are being transformed every second into light and heat.

3.10 Friction

If you give an object a push and send it sliding over the floor it slows down and comes to rest. The force applied in your push gave the object an acceleration, but when the force ceased, the object started slowing down. But objects should continue in motion with a uniform velocity. Why does the sliding object slow down when we stop pushing? We say the answer is *friction*. Forces are acting on a sliding object, even when we stop pushing.

The forces are the forces of friction. Such forces always oppose relative motion between two surfaces. So when an object slides across the floor there is an opposing force, that of friction, acting in opposition to the motion and so producing a negative acceleration, a reduction in velocity.

The friction between bodies depends on a number of factors. For example, it is easier to slide a book rather than a large heavy packing case along the floor. Weight thus might be a factor. It is easier to slide a block of ice rather than a block of wood, even if it is the same weight. Thus, the nature of the material would seem to be a factor. A simple way of investigating these factors is to measure the forces needed to slide a block over a surface. Figure 3.12 shows a possible arrangement. The force necessary to just start

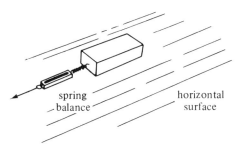

spring balance   horizontal surface

Fig. 3.12

the object moving is measured. When the object just starts to move then we must have a net force acting on the object. Up to that point the frictional force must have been equal to the pull force. Only when the pull force becomes larger than the frictional force does motion occur. Suppose we measure this force to start motion for the block with different masses placed on top of it, so that the force pressing the block against the surface is changed. Experimental results show that the force needed to cause motion is directly proportional to the force pushing the block against the surface. This is true even if the surface on which the sliding occurs is not horizontal. The force pushing the two surfaces together is called the normal force, N. If the normal force is doubled then the force necessary to cause motion is doubled.

force necessary to cause motion $\propto$ normal force

The force necessary to cause motion is the maximum value of the frictional force. Once that value has been passed then there is force left over to cause motion. So we can write

maximum frictional force $\propto$ normal force

$$F \propto N$$

The frictional force also depends on the nature of the two materials between which sliding occurs. There is, however, one factor which does not change the frictional force, that is the area where the two surfaces are in contact. If we measure the force needed to start motion with a block on one of its surfaces,

47

and then turn the block on to a side to give a different area in contact, then the force needed to start motion is unchanged. Friction does not depend on the area where the two surfaces are in contact.

The only two factors thus affecting the frictional force are the normal force and the nature of the materials concerned. With some materials the frictional force might be half the normal force, in other cases it might be only 0·3 of the normal force. The fraction depends on the materials concerned.

In one case

$$\frac{F}{N} = \frac{1}{2} = 0\cdot5$$

and another

$$\frac{F}{N} = 0\cdot3$$

The ratio of the frictional force to the normal force is called the *coefficient of friction* μ.

$$\frac{F}{N} = \mu$$

or by multiplying both sides of the expression by N we have

$$F = \mu N$$

The frictional force is proportional to the normal force and depends on the value of μ.

For a book sliding on a table μ is typically about 0·3. So if the book has a weight of 5 N, i.e., a mass of about 0·5 kg, then the force needed to start motion is $0\cdot3 \times 0\cdot5 = 0\cdot15$ N. A dry car tyre on a dry road gives a coefficient of friction of about 1·0. This means that the force needed to cause sliding is the same as the normal force. In the case of a car with four wheels the normal force will be one-quarter of the weight of the car. When this force is applied to the tyre then sliding, i.e., skidding can occur. For a car with a mass of 2000 kg, this is a weight of 20 000 N and so a force of 5000 N is needed for sliding. For a wet tyre on a wet road the coefficient of friction is about 0·2. The force needed to cause sliding, i.e., skidding, is thus $0\cdot2 \times 5000 = 1000$ N. Thus, on a wet road the force needed to cause skidding is only 1/5 that on a dry road.

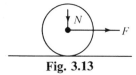

Fig. 3.13

It is harder to start a body moving than to keep it moving. The force needed to start a body sliding is called the static frictional force, and gives us a *static coefficient of friction*. The force needed to keep an object moving

48

with a uniform velocity, i.e., just to balance out the frictional force, is called the kinetic frictional force and gives us a *kinetic coefficient of friction*. There are other coefficients of friction, e.g., in the case of rolling. It is easier to roll an object than slide it—hence the wide use of the wheel. The coefficient in this case is defined as the ratio of the force applied at the centre of the roller (Fig. 3.13) to the normal force.

$$\mu_R = \frac{F}{N}$$

For a rubber tyre on a road the rolling coefficient of friction is only about 0·05. For $N = 5000$ N, then F is only 250 N. This is a lot less than the force needed to cause sliding, i.e., 5000 N, and so the conclusion is reached that it is easier to roll the wheel than slide it.

The high forces needed to start sliding with a car tyre are important. If the forces were not so high it would be impossible either to apply the brakes and come rapidly to a standstill, or to accelerate rapidly away from rest. In both these cases high forces are applied and the result is only successful if no sliding occurs. Thus braking forces can be applied, without sliding occurring, up to 5000 N on a dry road and 1000 N on a wet road.

The interaction between a car tyre and the road, between your shoes and the floor, are examples of where friction is desirable. In machinery friction is generally undesirable. Friction in bearings means that a force has to be used to overcome friction before useful work can be done. When you rub your hands together you can feel the action of frictional forces; there is also the result that your hands become warm. Because you are moving your hands against the frictional forces energy has to be used, work has to be done. This energy is transformed into heat. When a bearing rotates the effect of friction is to produce heat. Thus all the energy input to the machine does not appear as the output, but some part of it is wasted as heat. The *efficiency* of the machine is not 100 per cent. We define efficiency as

$$\text{efficiency} = \frac{\text{useful output energy}}{\text{total input energy}} \times 100 \text{ per cent}$$

About 30 per cent of the energy from the petrol in a car is used in overcoming friction, the waste energy appearing as heat from the engine and the radiator.

If you rub your hands together for some time you might rub pieces of skin off, i.e., your hands might experience wear. This is another undesirable aspect of friction. Wear and energy losses cost money. Careful design to reduce frictional forces can save money.

3.11 Stretching materials

If one end of a strip of rubber is held in a clamp and I pull on the other end, a force, my pull, moves through a distance as the rubber stretches under the action of the force. Energy is transferred from me to the rubber. If the stretched rubber is released the energy can be released by the rubber—if it twangs back and hits you the energy transfer from the rubber to you will be very apparent. When you pull a strip of rubber, or a spring, the force changes as you pull, getting bigger the more you pull. Figure 3.14 shows a

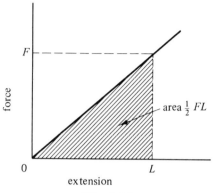

Fig. 3.14

possible force–extension graph, the force being in this case directly proportional to the extension. We can calculate the energy needed for the extension, by say a length L, by working out the average force needed to produce the extension. This will be $\frac{1}{2}F$, where F is the force needed for the extension L. The energy needed is thus $\frac{1}{2}FL$, i.e., average force × distance. But $\frac{1}{2}FL$ is the area under the force–extension graph up to the force F. In fact, whatever the shape of the force–extension graph we can calculate the energy needed by determining the area under the graph.

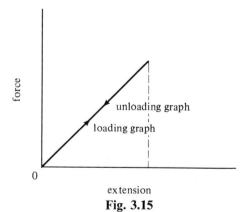

Fig. 3.15

If when we release the stretched piece of rubber the force–extension graph is just the same as when the rubber was stretched (Fig. 3.15) then all the energy transferred to the rubber during the stretching is released. If, however, on releasing the rubber the material does not return via the same

50

force–extension graph as when the specimen was pulled, then not all the energy put into the rubber during the stretching is returned in the form of movement of the end of the strip of rubber (the twang part). In other words, if you make a catapult out of the rubber and use energy to pull the catapult rubber back, not all this energy will appear as kinetic energy of the stone in the catapult when the rubber is released. Some part of the energy appears as heat. The amount that appears as heat is the difference in areas under the force–extension graph when the rubber is being extended and when it is released; Fig. 3.16.

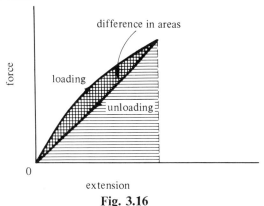

Fig. 3.16

When a car has been driven for some distance, then the tyre feels warm. This is because each part of the tyre, as it comes into contact with the road, is compressed and, when it moves on, it becomes extended back to its original dimensions. Because the force–distance graph for the rubber used in car tyres is not the same for loading and unloading, energy becomes wasted as heat.

Appendix: Powers

A million is 1 000 000, i.e., a one with six noughts after it. We might come across the need to write the number for two hundred thousand million, 200 000 000 000. Such large numbers do occur frequently in science and the technologies. It does, however, get rather cumbersome writing such numbers out in full. One possible way of shortening the task is to refer to the number, in this case 2, and the number of noughts that follow it. In this case we have 2 followed by 11 noughts. There is, however, another way of writing such numbers, using what are called powers.

$$
\begin{aligned}
10 & \\
100 &= 10 \times 10 \\
1000 &= 10 \times 10 \times 10 \\
10\,000 &= 10 \times 10 \times 10 \times 10 \\
100\,000 &= 10 \times 10 \times 10 \times 10 \times 10 \\
1\,000\,000 &= 10 \times 10 \times 10 \times 10 \times 10 \times 10
\end{aligned}
$$

A hundred is the product of two tens, a thousand is the product of three tens, ten thousand is the product of four tens, and so on. In order to indicate that a hundred is the product of two tens we can write it as 10^2. A thousand is the product of three tens and so is 10^3. A million is the product of six tens and so is 10^6.

$$10 = 10^1$$
$$100 = 10^2$$
$$1000 = 10^3$$
$$10\ 000 = 10^4$$
$$100\ 000 = 10^5$$
$$1\ 000\ 000 = 10^6$$

Our number 200 000 000 000 is two times 100 000 000 000 and so is written as 2×10^{11}.

$$1400 = 14 \times 100 \quad = 14 \times 10^2$$
$$= 1{\cdot}4 \times 1000 = 1{\cdot}4 \times 10^3$$

For numbers smaller than one, the same type of notation can still be used.

$$0{\cdot}1 = \frac{1}{10} \quad = 10^{-1}$$

$$0{\cdot}01 = \frac{1}{100} \quad = 10^{-2}$$

$$0{\cdot}001 = \frac{1}{1000} = 10^{-3}$$

The minus sign in front of the power indicates that we are dealing with one divided by a number of tens.

A rectangle with sides of 3 cm and 4 cm has an area of $3 \times 4 = 12$ square centimetres. Square centimetres are the units we arrive at when we multiply centimetres by centimetres. When we multiply ten by ten we call the product 10^2. Similarly, when we multiply centimetres by centimetres we call the product centimetre², or cm².

A box has a base 3 cm by 4 cm and a height of 2 cm. The volume of the box is $3 \times 4 \times 2 = 24$ cubic centimetres. This unit is cm × cm × cm, and can be written as cm³.

Problems

Describing motion

1. A car travels 5 km in 4 minutes. What was its average speed over that time?
2. A car averages a speed of 80 km/h for 3 h.
   (a) How far does it travel in those 3 h?

(b) How far might you expect it to have travelled in one of those hours? Why can you not be certain of the answer?

3. The velocity of a car is 50 km/h due north. Where will the car be 2 h after it starts?

4. The velocity of a car changes by 10 km/h in 2 min. What is the average acceleration in units of km/h per min?

5. If the average acceleration of an object is 4 m/s² by how much does its velocity change in (a) 1 s, (b) 5 s?

Units

6. If distance was measured in units of millimetres and time in hours, what would be the unit of velocity?

7. Convert a velocity of 50 km/h into units of (a) m/h, (b) m/s.

Graphically describing motion

8. The following distance–time data refer to the motion of a train. Plot the data as a distance–time graph and describe the type of motion occurring.

Distance in km	0	25	50	75	100	125	150
Time in s	0	1200	2000	2500	3600	5000	6000

9. For the data in question 8 estimate
   (a) the average speed for the entire journey,
   (b) the average speed over the first 25 km,
   (c) the maximum speed reached.

10. Sketch a distance–time graph for an object moving with a uniform velocity.

11. The following velocity–time data refer to the motion of a car. The velocities are the speedometer readings at the times stated. Plot a velocity–time graph and describe the type of motion occurring.

Velocity in m/s	0	2	4	6	8	10	12	14
Time in s	0	1·0	2·0	2·7	3·3	4·1	4·3	4·3

12. What is the average acceleration, for the data in question 11, over the first 10 s? At what time was the acceleration the greatest?

Equations describing motion

13. $v_1 = v_0 + at$
   (a) Explain the meaning of the symbols in the above equation.
   (b) What does the *at* term represent?

14. A car starts from rest and accelerates at a uniform acceleration of 1·5 m/s² for 10 s.
   (a) What is the velocity of the car at the end of that time?
   (b) How far does the car travel in the time?

15. A sportscar accelerates uniformly from rest to 44 m/s in 6 s, and then brakes to come to rest with a uniform deceleration in 4 s. How far does the car travel from start to finish?

Reaction time

16. If your reaction time was 0·5 s and you were travelling in a car at 60 km/h, how far would you travel before your foot hit the brake pedal?
17. Suppose the brakes of a car cause the car to decelerate at the uniform rate of 4 m/s². How long would it take for the car to come to rest from a velocity of 60 km/h?
18. Suppose your reaction time was 1·0 s, and you were travelling in a car moving with a velocity of 100 km/h, and that application of the brakes causes a uniform deceleration of 5 m/s². How far would the car travel between your seeing some event causing you to react, and the car coming to a standstill?

Forces and motion

19. If an object is at rest then the net force on the object must be zero. Explain the reason for the word *net*.
20. Calculate the acceleration given to a mass of 3 kg by
    (a) a force of 2 N,
    (b) a force of 10 N,
    (c) zero force.
21. Explain what is meant by the term *inertia*.
22. Figure 3.17 shows a length of ticker tape that was attached at one end to a moving object. As the object moved it pulled the tape through a vibrator that put dots on the tape every 1/50 s. Thus the time between successive dots is 1/50 s. Use the results given by the tape to plot a graph showing how the position of the moving object varied with time.

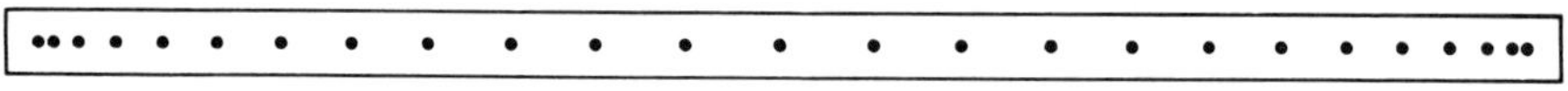

Fig. 3.17

23. Figure 3.18 shows a chart made by cutting up a length of ticker tape into ten *tick* lengths. A *tick* is the time interval between successive dots, i.e., 1/50 s. Successive lengths of the tape are mounted side by side. A cut length of tape thus represents the distance covered in ten ticks, i.e., the average velocity. How does the average velocity change for the example given in the figure?
24. Which of the tape charts in Fig. 3.19 has been produced by an object moving with the greatest acceleration? How can you tell that the acceleration in each case was uniform?

Free fall

25. Determine from Fig. 3.8 the acceleration due to gravity.

26. A freely falling object falls with an acceleration of about 10 m/s².
    (a) Starting from rest, what will be the velocity after 1 s?
    (b) By how much will the velocity change in the second second? Hence determine the velocity after 2 s.
    (c) By how much will the velocity change in the third second? Hence determine the velocity after 3 s.

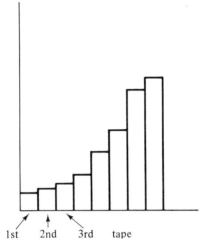

1st   2nd   3rd   tape

Fig. 3.18

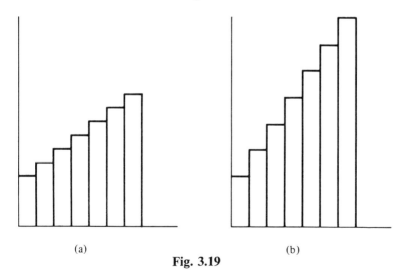

(a)   (b)

Fig. 3.19

27. This follows on from the previous question.
    (a) What is the average velocity during the first second of free fall?
    (b) What is the distance fallen in the first second?
    (c) What is the average velocity over the first two seconds of free fall?
    (d) What is the distance covered during the first two seconds?

(e) What is the average velocity over the first three seconds?

(f) What is the distance covered during the first three seconds?

28. What is the gravitational force acting on a mass of (a) 1 kg, (b) 5 kg? Give your answer in newtons.

Energy

29. (a) What is the gravitational force acting on an object of mass 3 kg? Take *g* to be about 10 m/s².

(b) If you lift the object, against what force are you moving it during the lifting?

(c) If you lift the object 2 m how much energy is needed?

30. Suppose we have an object attached to one end of a spring, the other end of the spring being held in a clamp. When the object is pulled through a distance of 2 cm the average force exerted by the spring is 10 N. What is the energy needed to pull the object through this distance?

31. A stone is placed in the rubber of a catapult. The stone is then pulled back against the rubber. To do this an average force of 40 N is needed to pull the rubber back 1 cm. What is the energy needed?

Conservation of energy

32. Write notes giving an explanation of the principle of conservation of energy for a fellow student who missed the appropriate class.

33. What is the potential energy given to an object of mass 2 kg when lifted through a vertical height of (a) 1 m, (b) 3 m?

34. What is the sequence of energy transformations involved in

(a) a petrol-driven motor running a hoist lifting bricks?

(b) a bouncing ball?

Power

35. What is the power when energy is transformed at the rate of

(a) 50 J in 10 s,

(b) 1200 J in 1 min?

36. How many joules of energy are transformed every second by an electric fire operating at 1 kW?

Friction

37. A force of 20 N is needed to start an object sliding on a horizontal surface. What is the value of the frictional force?

38. An object has a weight of 50 N, and a force of 20 N is needed to start the object sliding on a horizontal surface. What is the coefficient of static friction?

39. The coefficient of static friction for steel sliding on steel is 0·7. For a steel block of weight 10 N, what force is needed to start it sliding on a horizontal steel surface?

40. The coefficient of friction for brake material on the brake drum of a car is greater than one, about 1·2 when dry. What is the significance of the value being greater than one?

41. If the efficiency of an engine is rated as 15 per cent, how much of a 1000 J energy intake would you expect to find as useful output energy?

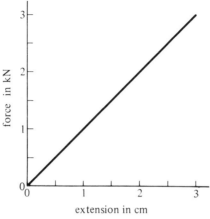

Fig. 3.20

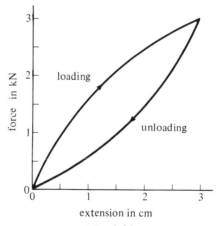

Fig. 3.21

Stretching materials

42. Estimate the energy used to stretch, by 2 cm, the material whose force–extension graph is shown in Fig. 3.20.

43. Estimate the energy dissipated when the material, whose force–extension graph is shown in Fig. 3.21, is stretched and then released.

Discussion points

1. The science and technology relating to friction is called tribology. Tribological mismanagement is said to cost industry large sums of money. For example, a reduction in friction at a bearing reduces both the power wasted and wear, and so could mean that the bearing can be used without replacement for a much longer time. Tribological mismanagement means that design is not taking into account frictional effects in order to reduce running costs. Taking frictional effects into account may mean a higher initial cost, but lower running costs might result. Consider some machines with which you are familiar and the breakdowns that occur. Are they due to frictional effects? Would better design have helped?

2. The world's stock of fossil fuels is considered to be rapidly running out. In newspaper headlines this may appear as a statement that the world's energy resources are running out. What will be the possible effects of a run down in the stocks of fossil fuels?

Background reading

Ubbelohde, A. R., *Man and Energy*, Penguin, 1963. Chapter 3, in particular, is relevant to discussion point (2) above.

Stone, R., and R. Dennien, 'Energy', *Physics Topics*, Longman, 1974. Useful background reading on energy and power.

Harrison, R. D., 'Forces', *Physics Topics*, Longman, 1968. Useful background reading on forces.

Chapman, P., *Fuels Paradise, Energy Options for Britain*, Penguin, 1975. Useful information source for discussion point (2) above.

4. Fluids

4.1 Pressure

Around 1960 the fashion in ladies' shoes was for stiletto heels. Such heels were very small in the area in contact with the ground, a typical area being of the order of 12 mm². These heels caused considerable damage to floors and, in some cases, were banned because of the damage caused. Cork and wood floors were particularly badly damaged. Why should these heels cause more concern than the heels of other types of shoes? The gravitational force with which a person presses against the floor is the same whether they are in stocking feet or wearing stiletto heels; Fig. 4.1.

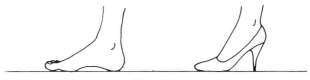

Fig. 4.1

The mass of a typical woman is probably about 60 kg. The gravitational force acting on her is thus about 600 N, i.e., 60 kgf. With stiletto heels this force presses down on two heels, each being in contact with an area of the floor of 12 mm². The force on each square millimetre is thus

$$\frac{600}{2 \times 12} = 25 \text{ N per mm}^2$$

I have assumed that all the weight is taken by the heels and none by the soles of the shoes being in contact with the ground.

The heel of a man's shoe is typically about 5000 mm². For the same weight, 600 N, this gives a force per square millimetre of

$$\frac{600}{2 \times 5000} = 0 \cdot 06 \text{ N per mm}^2$$

The force per square millimetre with a stiletto heel is considerably greater than that with a man's shoe. Because in many instances it is important to know the force per unit area a name is given to the quantity. *Pressure* is defined as the force per unit area.

$$\text{Pressure} = \frac{\text{force}}{\text{area}}$$

The units of pressure are the units of force divided by those of area, e.g., N/m^2. A unit frequently used in place of the N/m^2 is the pascal (Pa). One pascal is one newton per square metre.

A block of metal acted on by a gravitational force of 2 N and having a base area in contact with the floor of 1 cm^2 exerts a pressure on the floor of 2 N/cm^2.

4.2 Liquid pressure

A solid presses downwards on the floor on which it rests and so exerts a pressure on the floor. The solid presses down against the floor because of the force of gravity on the solid. Liquids also have mass and so gravity acts on them. Thus, in a beaker of liquid, there is a force acting on the base of the liquid due to the mass of liquid above the base. Hence the liquid exerts a pressure on the base of the beaker.

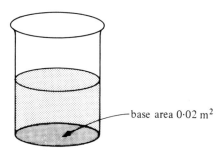

—base area 0·02 m^2

Fig. 4.2

Suppose there was 0·2 kg of liquid in a beaker (Fig. 4.2) with a base area of 0·02 m^2. The gravitational force acting on this mass of liquid is 0·2 kgf or 2 N. Hence the pressure is

$$\frac{2}{0·02} = 100 \text{ N/m}^2$$

Suppose that in the beaker in Fig. 4.2 we had a height h of liquid of density d, the area of the base of the beaker being A. The volume of the liquid will be $A \times d$. As

$$\text{mass} = \text{density} \times \text{volume}$$

the total mass of liquid in the beaker will be $d \times A \times h$. The gravitational force acting on this mass is given by multiplying the mass by a factor near to 10, this converts the mass into a gravitational force in newtons. The factor near to 10 is the acceleration due to gravity g (see chapter 3). So the gravitational force acting on the liquid is $d \times A \times h \times g$. This force acts over an area A and so the pressure acting on the base is

$$\frac{d \times A \times h \times g}{A} = dhg$$

The pressure on the base, due to the liquid above it, is proportional to the density d, the height h and the acceleration due to gravity g. If the height of the liquid in the beaker is doubled then the pressure is doubled. If the density of the liquid in the beaker is increased to twice the initial value then the pressure is doubled.

Water has a density of 1000 kg/m³, thus the pressure on the base of a beaker under 0·01 m of water is

$$\text{pressure} = dhg = 1000 \times 0·01 \times 10$$
$$= 100 \text{ N/m}^2$$

If the liquid height had been 0·02 m then the pressure would have been 200 N/m²; doubling the height doubles the pressure.

Mercury has a density of 13 600 kg/m³, and so a beaker of mercury to a depth of 0·01 m has a pressure acting on the base of

$$13\ 600 \times 0·01 \times 10 = 1360 \text{ N/m}^2$$

Because of the greater density the pressure on the base is greater than that produced by the same depth of water.

4.3 Water finds its own level

There is a saying that water finds its own level. If you dig a hole on a beach or in soil near a river, then water seeps in until the level of the water in the hole is the same as the level of the water in the sea or river. Why does the water seep in? What forces cause it to move? What determines the level to which the water rises?

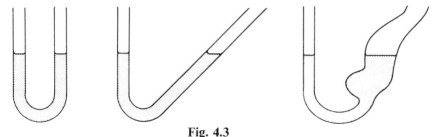

Fig. 4.3

Figure 4.3 shows a number of U-tubes into which water has been poured. It does not matter which limb of the U-tube the water is poured into first, or how much water is used, the level of the water in one limb of the U is always the same as the level in the other limb. This is true regardless of the shape of the limbs.

We can calculate the pressure at the base of a column of liquid by using the equation $p = dhg$. This equation does not involve the area of cross-section of a limb, but only the height of the liquid, its density, and g. With the same liquid in each limb then d is the same, also g, and so the same height means the same pressure at the base of the limb. The shape of the limb obviously plays no part in determining the pressure at the base of a column of liquid.

When the water is poured into one of the limbs of the U-tube we may have, for a short period of time, a greater level in one limb than the other. The water, however, rapidly flows between the limbs until the levels in each limb are the same. When the levels in the two limbs are different then there are different pressures at the base of each column. The water flows between the limbs to equalize the pressures. If we pour water into a can which has a hole near the base (Fig. 4.4) then the water spurts out. The pressure at that point under the water surface causes the water to spurt out. The pressure, at the base of the U-tube, within the water in the U-tube causes the water to

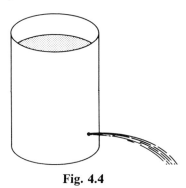

Fig. 4.4

move between limbs until the pressures are the same at the same level. These facts suggest that the pressure at any level in a liquid acts equally in all directions. If there is at the same level, say the level of the base of the U-tube, a difference in pressure then the liquid flows until the pressures are the same. When there is no net motion at any horizontal level then the pressure is at that level everywhere the same.

The water seeping into the hole on the beach does so because it is driven by a pressure difference between the water in the bottom of the hole and that in the sea at the same horizontal level. We can summarize these points as:

The pressure at a point in a fluid is the same in all directions.

The pressure at all points at the same horizontal level, in a fluid at rest, is the same.

4.4 Hydraulics

If you fill a polythene container with water, close it, and squeeze the container, the water in the container is subject to a pressure. If the container has holes in it (Fig. 4.5) then the water spurts out in all directions. The container is perhaps only squeezed at one corner, but the water still spurts out in all directions from the various holes. Liquids are very difficult to compress and so, if squashed in one region, the liquid tends to come out in another direction. This demonstrates that a pressure exerted at one place on a liquid in a closed vessel is transmitted throughout the liquid.

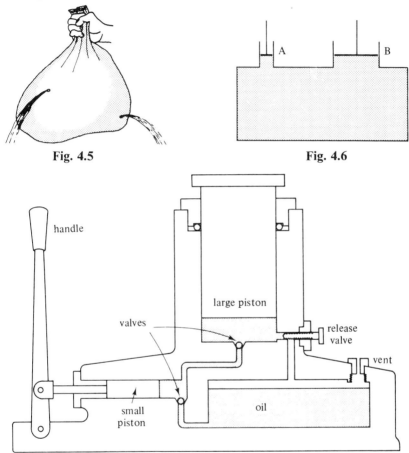

Fig. 4.5

Fig. 4.6

Fig. 4.7 Hydraulic jack

Figure 4.6 shows a simplified sketch of a hydraulic press. A force applied to one of the pistons causes pressure to be applied to the fluid. This pressure is then transmitted through the fluid to the other piston, and is able to cause that piston to move. If a force of 50 N is applied to piston A and it has a cross-sectional area of 1 cm^2, then the pressure applied to the liquid is 50 N per cm^2. This is the pressure communicated throughout the fluid and is, thus, the pressure acting on piston B. But, if piston B has a cross-sectional area of 10 cm^2, then the total force acting on it will be 500 N. The hydraulic press thus enables large forces to be produced by the use of quite small forces.

This principle is used in the hydraulic jack; Fig. 4.7. Force is applied to a small piston by means of a lever. The pressure is then transmitted through a fluid to a large piston and results in movement of that piston.

When a pressure acts on a surface the force experienced by the surface is always at right-angles to the surface.

4.5 Gas pressure

If we take a U-tube and put water into it then the levels of the water in the two limbs will come to the same level. The pressure at the base of each limb is thus the same. If, however, we connect one side of the U-tube to the gas supply (Fig. 4.8), and open the gas tap, then the levels of the water in the two limbs no longer remains the same. The water level on the side connected to the gas supply is lower than on the side open to the atmosphere. The pressure at the base of the U-tube, however, must still be the same, and so we are left to conclude that the gas is exerting a pressure which is equivalent to that

connection to
gas supply

Fig. 4.8

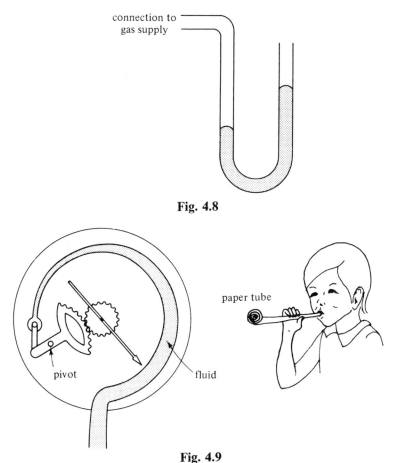

paper tube

pivot

fluid

Fig. 4.9

64

given by a column of water equal to the difference between the two water levels. By the use of a U-tube, containing water, or more commonly mercury, gas pressures can be measured. Such a device is called a *manometer*.

Another instrument that can be used for the measurement of pressure is the Bourdon gauge. The rolled paper tube type of toy that you blow into and it straightens out is based on the same principle as the Bourdon gauge; Fig. 4.9. When the pressure in the curved tube increases the tube tries to straighten out and, in doing this, moves a pointer across a scale.

4.6 Atmospheric pressure

If we had a U-tube in which the level of mercury on one side was 760 mm higher than the level on the other side, we would conclude that on the lower level side there was a pressure acting on the surface of the mercury equivalent to a column of mercury 760 mm high; Fig. 4.10.

If a thick-walled glass tube about a metre long, sealed at one end, is held vertically and filled with mercury (Fig. 4.11) we have a mercury column about

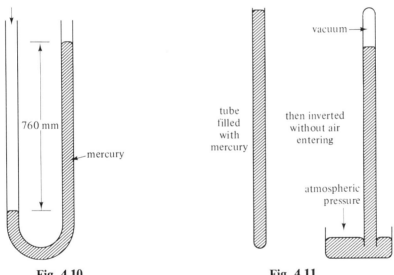

Fig. 4.10   Fig. 4.11

1 m long. If a thumb is placed over the open end and the tube is then inverted into a trough of mercury, removal of the thumb under the mercury surface allows no air to enter the tube. The situation is rather like a U-tube with the open mercury surface in the trough being one side of the U, and the mercury in the glass tube the other side. We might expect the level in the tube to drop to the same level as that in the trough—it does not. The level of mercury in the tube drops until the level is about 760 mm above the level in the trough. This must mean that there is a pressure on the mercury level in the trough equivalent to that of a column of mercury 760 mm high.

This pressure is what we call the *atmospheric pressure*. The space above the mercury in the tube contains no air, it is a vacuum. This apparatus is called a *mercury barometer*, and is one method by which the atmospheric pressure may be measured.

The atmospheric pressure is roughly equivalent to that produced by putting a mass of 1 kg on an area of one square centimetre. This is about 10 N/cm^2, or 10^5 N/m^2, or 10^5 Pa (see section 4.1). The atmospheric pressure depends on weather conditions and also on the altitude above sea level at which the measurement is made. One method of determining altitude is to measure the atmospheric pressure. The atmospheric pressure at the altitude at which a passenger aircraft might fly, about 6000 m, is only about half the atmospheric pressure at sea level. The atmospheric pressure decreases with altitude because the higher you go the less air there is above you, and so the smaller is the gravitational force acting on that air mass above, and hence the smaller the pressure. It is like having a vertical pile of bricks. The pressure acting on the bottom brick is due to the gravitational force of all the bricks above it. This is obviously less for a brick higher up in the pile, because there are less bricks above it.

4.7 Dams

A civil engineer who designs a dam needs to calculate the forces resulting from pressures due to water. The water depth behind a dam may be as much as 300 m and the pressure at this depth is high. The density of water is about 1000 kg/m^3, and the acceleration due to gravity is about 10 m/s^2, so that

$$\text{Pressure} = dhg = 300 \times 1000 \times 10$$

This gives the pressure as 3 000 000 N/m^2, i.e., three million newtons per square metre. This is the pressure due to the 300 m of water. On top of this we need to add the pressure at the water surface due to the atmospheric pressure, about 100 000 N/m^2. The total pressure is thus about 3 100 000 N/m^2. This is the pressure acting on the base of the dam; the pressure acting on the dam at the water surface will only be 100 000 N/m^2, i.e., the atmospheric pressure.

At a depth of 150 m, i.e., half the full depth, the pressure is 150 000 N/m^2 due to the water. At 75 m the pressure is 75 000 N/m^2. The pressure acting on the dam varies with the water depth, and is greatest at the base of the dam. The forces acting on the dam thus increase as the depth increases.

Problems

Pressure

1. A force of 50 N acts over an area of 2 m^2. What is the pressure?
2. Why on thin ice is it safer to lie down on the ice rather than stand up?

3. Why for movement over soft ground is it useful for a bulldozer to have caterpillar tracks?
4. Why do knives with sharp blades cut more easily than knives with blunt blades?
5. Estimate the pressure exerted by you when using a knife to cut an object.

Liquid pressure
6. Why does water spurt out of a hole in the bottom of a water tank? Does the water spurt out with the same force if the hole is half-way up the tank?
7. Why, in a house, is the cold water tank placed as high as possible?
8. Calculate the pressure at a depth of 100 m under water of density 1000 kg/m³. Take the acceleration due to gravity as 10 m/s², and consider only the pressure due to the water.
9. What is the pressure at the base of a column of mercury 760 mm high, if the density of mercury is 13 600 kg/m³? Take the acceleration due to gravity to be 9·8 m/s².

Water finds its own level
10. Explain what is implied by the phrase 'water finds its own level', for a fellow student who missed the class in which the topic was discussed.
11. What happens if there is a pressure difference between two points in a fluid at the same horizontal level?

Hydraulics
12. A hydraulic press has pistons of area 20 cm² and 160 cm². If a force of 100 N is applied to the smaller piston, what will be the force acting on the larger piston?
13. A hydraulic press in which the force applied at the input is less than the force produced at the output might seem to be a way of getting something for nothing. Do you get something for nothing? What about the conservation of energy?

Gas pressure
14. Why, when measuring a small pressure difference with a manometer, is water a reasonable fluid to use, but when larger pressures are involved mercury is better?
15. The two levels in a water manometer differ by 5 cm. What is the pressure difference between the two sides in N/m²? Take the density of water as 1000 kg/m³ and the acceleration due to gravity as 10 m/s².
16. What would the pressure difference have been in question 15 if the fluid in the manometer had been mercury instead of water? Take the density of mercury to be 13 600 kg/m³.

Atmospheric pressure

17. Atmospheric pressure is measured with an instrument called a barometer. It is usual to quote the pressure as 'so many centimetres or millimetres of mercury'. What would be the pressure in N/m^2 if the pressure was 760 mm of mercury? Take the density of mercury to be 13 600 kg/m^3 and the acceleration due to gravity as 10 m/s^2.

18. The pressure due to the atmosphere is about 10 N/cm^2.
    (a) What is the force acting on the upper surface of a shelf 50 cm long by 20 cm wide?
    (b) What is the force acting on the lower surface of the shelf? Assume the shelf to be thin.
    (c) Why does the shelf not collapse under the action of the atmospheric pressure?
    (d) If the 50 cm by 20 cm surface were the upper surface of the lid of a box in which there was a vacuum, what would be the force acting on the upper and inner surfaces of the lid?

19. On a day when a mercury barometer stands at a height of 760 mm, what would be the height of a barometer in which water was used in place of mercury? Density of water = 1000 kg/m^3, density of mercury = 13 600 kg/m^3.

Dams

20. What would be the highest pressure acting on a dam for a reservoir with a maximum depth of 100 metres? Take the density of water to be 1000 kg/m^3 and the acceleration due to gravity as 10 m/s^2.

Discussion points

Water is essential in any community, but particularly in a modern technological society. To produce a 1000 kg of steel, something of the order of 300 000 kg of water is needed. The average water consumption per person in a British city is about 140 kg per day; in a warmer drier climate such as in parts of the United States the consumption can be as high as four times that figure. These figures are arrived at by dividing the total water consumption by a city, this includes both domestic and industrial use, by the number of inhabitants of the city. The building of reservoirs, and the tapping of streams or underground supplies, have to increase year by year as populations increase in number, and also become more technological and affluent. What are the problems involved in obtaining adequate water supplies, and in getting the water to the consumer?

Background reading

Duff, A., 'Pressures', *Physics Topics*, Longman, 1969.

5. Heat

5.1 Temperature

We measure temperature by means of instruments called thermometers. The commonest thermometer is the mercury-in-glass thermometer. This consists of mercury in a sealed tube, the position of the upper level of the mercury being taken as a measure of the temperature; Fig. 5.1. The scale alongside the mercury level is marked in units called degrees. If the degrees are measured on what is called the Celsius scale, they are written as 20°C. This is a temperature of 20 degrees on the Celsius scale. This is about the temperature in a nicely warm room. Melting ice is 0°C, boiling water about 100°C.

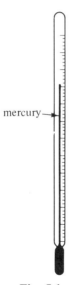

mercury

Fig. 5.1

Temperatures are measured by putting the thermometer in good contact with the substance whose temperature is required. Then, after a suitable period of waiting, the thermometer and the substance are assumed to have come to the same temperature and, so, the temperature of the substance can be taken as the temperature indicated by the thermometer. We talk of the substance and the thermometer coming into thermal equilibrium; Fig. 5.2.

If we take a block of ice out of a deep freeze and put a thermometer in contact with it, we may find that the temperature is −15°C. If we record the temperature of the ice and observe how it varies with time, a graph something like that in Fig. 5.3 will be produced. The temperature of the ice rises steadily until we reach 0°C, then it seems to 'stick' for a while before commencing to rise steadily again. At this 'sticking' temperature the ice is melting; above 0°C it is no longer ice but water. While the ice is changing into liquid water the temperature remains constant, at 0°C. This gives us a way of calibrating a thermometer. All we need to do is to put the thermometer in melting ice and mark the temperature as 0°C.

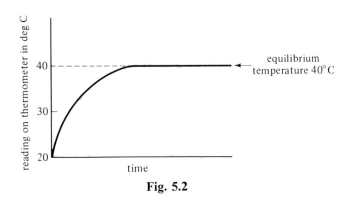

Fig. 5.2

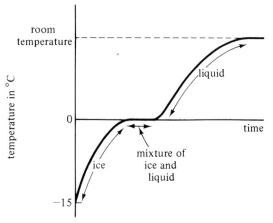

Fig. 5.3

If we use a thermometer to record the temperature of water when changing from liquid into steam (Fig. 5.4) we find that during the change the temperature remains constant. Under conditions where we boil water in an open beaker in the laboratory the temperature is generally 100°C. This is another fixed point by which we can calibrate a thermometer.

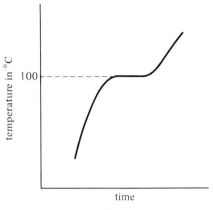

Fig. 5.4

With two such fixed points we can divide the interval between into 100 divisions, the degrees, and so produce a scale for a thermometer.

5.2 Heat as energy

Is heat a form of energy? When you rub your hands together they become warm. The energy of motion you gave your hands has, as a result of you moving one hand over the other against frictional forces, been converted into heat. If we believe that energy is always conserved, then the disappearance of the energy of motion and the appearance of heat can only be explained on the assumption that heat is a form of energy.

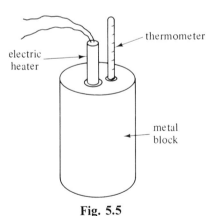

Fig. 5.5

A convenient way of obtaining heat energy is from an electric fire. Electric energy is transformed into heat energy. An electric current passing through a wire produces heat. If an electric fire is rated as 2 kW when connected to the 240 V mains supply, then this means that 2000 J of electrical energy are

71

used every second (see page 46). This is transformed into heat energy, and so we have 2000 J of heat energy produced every second.

What happens when we supply heat energy to a substance? It gets hotter, i.e., its temperature rises, or it might melt or evaporate, i.e., change state. But how big is the temperature rise for the energy supplied? How great a temperature rise is caused by 1 J of energy? One way of investigating this is to use a small electric heater which can be inserted in a hole in a block of metal, another hole holding a thermometer; Fig. 5.5. By either measuring the electrical energy input, or using the heater under specified conditions so that the energy output per second is known, we can supply known energy amounts to the metal block and find how the temperature changes.

The following are typical results for an electric heater which gave 50 J per second, i.e., its power was 50 W. The block is aluminium and has a mass of 1 kg.

Energy supplied in Joules (50 × time in seconds of running)	Temperature change in degrees Celsius
500	0·5
1000	1·1
1500	1·6
2000	2·1
2500	2·5

For each 500 J the temperature rises by about 0·5 degrees. The temperature rise is proportional to the energy supplied.

If we use a block of aluminium of twice the mass, we find that the temperature rise is still proportional to the energy supplied, but that the temperature rise is about 0·5 degrees for every 1000 J of energy. For twice the mass twice the amount of energy is needed to produce the same temperature rise. If we use three times the mass, we find that three times the energy is needed to give the same temperature rise. For a constant rise in temperature the energy needed is proportional to the mass.

If, instead of aluminium we use another substance, we find that the temperature rise per kilogramme of material depends on which material we are using. The energy needed to produce a temperature rise of 1 degree Celsius for a block of 1 kg is called the *specific heat capacity*. For aluminium the specific heat capacity is about 900 J per kg per deg C. The results in the table above indicate that 1000 J produced a temperature rise of 1·1 deg C with a block of 1 kg, in reasonable accord with the value quoted for the specific heat capacity.

We can represent these results as

energy supplied = specific heat capacity c × mass m × temperature rise θ

This equation fits the results that the temperature rise is proportional to the energy supplied, the mass and nature of the substance being constant; that the energy needed to produce the same temperature rise for a substance is proportional to the mass; and the definition of specific heat capacity.

The following table gives some typical specific heat capacities.

Substance	Specific heat capacity in J/kg/deg C
Aluminium	920
Steel	480
Copper	380
Water	4200

Compared with aluminium, much more energy is needed to raise the temperature of 1 kg of water by 1 deg C, but less energy is needed per kilogramme to raise the temperature of steel by 1 deg C.

How much energy is needed to raise the temperature of a 3 kg block of copper from 15 to 20°C?

$$\text{energy needed} = c \times m \times \theta$$
$$= 380 \times 3 \times 5$$
$$= 5700 \text{ J}$$

If the block had been made of aluminium the energy needed would have been:

$$\text{energy needed} = 920 \times 3 \times 5$$
$$= 13\,800 \text{ J}$$

More energy is needed because the specific heat capacity of aluminium is greater than that of copper.

5.3 Change of state

Energy is needed to change a substance from one state to another, e.g., from solid to liquid; this energy does not change the temperature. The amount of energy needed to change ice to liquid water can be determined by measuring the amount of ice at 0°C that is changed to water at 0°C by a certain measured energy input. Figure 5.6 shows a possible arrangement; a measured amount of electrical energy is fed to an electric heater immersed in melting ice, and the amount of ice melted is measured. To allow for the fact that some ice would melt during the course of the experiment, as a result of heat from the surroundings, a control experiment can be done measuring the amount of ice melted during the same time, without the heater being switched on. The results of such experiments show that about 334 000 J of energy are needed to change 1 kg of ice to liquid, without any change in temperature. Thus to change 2 kg of ice at 0°C to water at 0°C requires $2 \times 334\,000$ J. To change liquid water into steam, at 100°C, about 2 270 000 J are needed for every kilogramme. The amount of energy needed, per kilogramme, for a change of state, is called the *specific latent heat*.

Energy is needed to change from solid to liquid. When, however, a liquid changes to a solid this energy is released; it has to be removed for the change to take place. To condense steam there has to be a removal of energy. For every kilogramme of steam that is condensed 2 270 000 J have been removed.

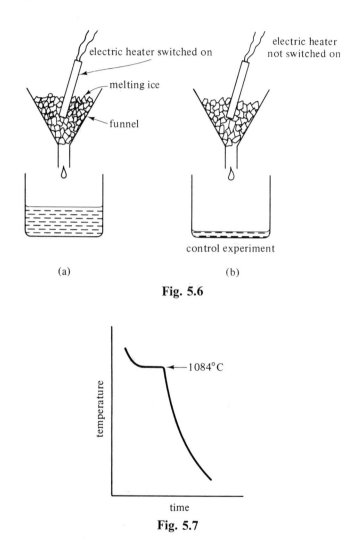

Fig. 5.6

Fig. 5.7

Figure 5.7 shows the cooling curve for copper when it cools from the liquid to the solid state. At the melting point of copper, 1084°C, the temperature remains constant because the normal cooling, the normal removal of energy, is balanced by the emission of energy as the copper solidifies. The specific latent heat of fusion of copper is about 206 000 J per kg.

Cooling curves for alloys do not show all the latent heat being released at one temperature, but the event occurring over a range of temperature. Figure 5.8 shows two such curves for different copper–nickel alloys. As the graphs indicate, the temperatures at which solidification starts and at which it ends indicate the relative amounts of the two elements present in the alloy.

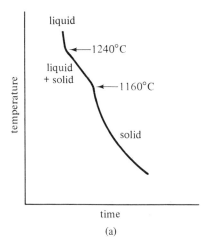

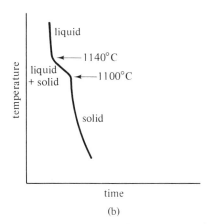

Fig. 5.8 (a) Cooling curve for an alloy of 30 per cent nickel and 70 per cent copper; (b) cooling curve for an alloy of 10 per cent nickel and 90 per cent copper

5.4 The effects of heat

What happens when we heat a solid? It expands. If we take a strip of steel at 20°C and heat it to 100°C, then the steel strip is longer at 100°C than at 20°C. A strip of steel 1 m long at 20°C will increase in length by almost 3 mm by the time it is at 100°C. A 1 m long strip of brass would have expanded by about 5 mm in going from 20°C to 100°C. If the length of the strip is doubled the amount it expands doubles. The amount of expansion depends also on the change in temperature. For very long lengths, quite a small change in temperature can produce very big changes in length.

One end of a bridge must be free to move so that expansion of the bridge can occur when temperatures rise. Figure 5.9 shows one way in which this can be achieved, the free end of the bridge resting on rollers and having a gap into which it can move. Expansion when the temperature rises is not restricted to metals, concrete expands also.

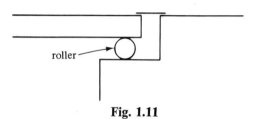

roller

Fig. 1.11

It is not only solids that expand when the temperature rises, liquids do as well. The thermometer depends on the expansion of a liquid, generally mercury. A glass bottle full of water at 20°C will be overflowing if the temperature rises. If, however, the bottle had been full of water at 0°C raising the temperature a little would have resulted in the water contracting, leaving room for more water to be added to the flask to keep it full. From 0°C to 4°C water contracts when the temperature rises, above that temperature it behaves like other liquids and expands when the temperature is increased.

Gases expand when heated, provided we allow them to expand and not just increase in gas pressure. 'Hot air rises' is a common phrase. The hot air rises because when the air is heated it expands. Because the same mass of air now occupies a larger volume its density must have decreased (density = mass/volume). Because all the colder air around is of a higher density the hot air rises, and the cold air falls. A hot air balloon depends for its lift on hot air being of lower density than cold air. The hot air in the balloon is produced by a burner directly under the lower open end of the balloon.

5.5 Transfer of heat

If you hold the end of a metal rod the other end of which is in a fire, you can soon tell that heat can be transferred along a metal rod. If you hold the end of a strip of wood the other end of which is in a fire, probably alight, then heat does not seem to be transferred along the strip to any significant extent. Metal conducts heat better than wood. We use the word *conduction* for the heat transfer that takes place through a solid. A pan on the electric, or gas, ring needs to be a good conductor of heat so that the heat is rapidly transferred through the pan from the hot element to the pan's contents. Hence pans are usually made of metal. The handle of the pan, however, needs to be a bad conductor of heat if you are to be able to lift a hot pan by the handle.

The heat spreads through the water in the pan. The movement of heat through the liquid is by a process called *convection*. The water near the bottom of the pan becomes hotter than the water above it. The hot water expands, and so the density of the hot water becomes less than the density of the cold water. The result is that the hot water rises and the cold water sinks. The heat is thus transferred to other parts of the water in the pan by the movement of hot liquid. Convection involves movement of the liquid. We can have convection with gases, the heat transfer being by movement of the hot gas.

There is another way in which heat can be transferred. The heat from the Sun warms us. This energy flow from the Sun is through the near-vacuum that lies between the Earth and the Sun. The heat flows from the Sun in the same way as light, indeed when there is an eclipse of the Sun both the heat and the light are cut off at the same moment. We call this method of heat transfer *radiation*. When you sit in front of an electric fire you can feel the heat by radiation, this is particularly true if the fire has a metal reflector behind the element; Fig. 5.10. The reflector reflects the radiation in the same way as it reflects light.

reflector

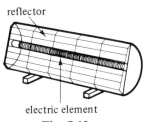

electric element

Fig. 5.10

5.6 Thermal insulation

Insulate and save fuel is the message of many advertisements; Fig. 5.11. The object, as far as a householder is concerned, is to reduce the amount of heat that escapes from the house to the surroundings. Heat energy costs money, and so the heat lost is wasted money. The heat losses from a house can be reduced by the use of suitable insulation.

Heat losses through the roof can be reduced by putting layers of glass fibre, or other similar material, in the roof space. Such insulators are essentially made up of lots of pockets of trapped air. Air is a poor conductor of heat and if trapped does not allow heat movement by convection currents. A string vest worn under a shirt works on a similar principle, air being trapped in the spaces between the meshes. Heat losses by conduction through the brick of the walls can be reduced by using cavity walls, i.e., two walls with an air gap between them. Again the air is used as a bad conductor of heat. Because convection currents can occur in the air in the cavity the insulation properties are considerably enhanced if a foam-like substance is pumped into the cavity to keep the air trapped in small pockets. Double glazing, i.e., two panes of glass separated by an air gap, can reduce the heat losses by conduction through windows. Mixing expanded mica with the concrete for the solid floor can reduce heat losses through the floor, again by trapping air.

Do this quick on-the-spot check in your factory today and find out to what extent your Company's wasting heat – and what you could do about it.

1. See if the operating controls of your heating system can be altered to achieve better control and distribution. Re-siting and a multi-time switch/thermostat arrangement could dramatically shorten the system's operating period without sacrificing anybody's comfort.

2. Review the operating temperature of the heating system. A reduction of a few degrees can result in very useful savings over the winter period – without anyone feeling the pinch.

3. As you walk through the factory, check if doors are open. Heat escaping this way costs a fortune, yet by installing automatic closures, screening, air curtains or personnel doors, for instance, you'd help keep the heat where it belongs – inside the building.

4. Inspect the roof, normally the greatest single source of uncontrolled heat loss. Uncontrollable ventilators, faulty under-glazing sealing strips and open jack roofs eat into company profits at the rate of £300 per sq. metre a year – and the cost is rising.

5. Check the temperature at roof level and compare it with the temperature at working level. A steeply-rising temperature gradient means excessive heat losses through the roof and inadequate heating for those working on the factory floor.

6. If you haven't done so already, consider which of your most competent engineers should be delegated the responsibility and authority for making specific savings in Company fuel costs – and make a point of regarding this important appointment as urgent.

If this brief random check shows you're wasting heat, get Colt to carry out a full, comprehensive survey of your buildings absolutely free of charge. Our Area Manager will work out what your heat losses cost and show you how the Colt Wastemaster system could help your Company achieve what hundreds have achieved already – a saving of up to 20% on factory heating bills. The survey could even include a study of the relative costs of operating your present fuel-consuming plant and purchasing new. (Frequently, savings can offset capital expenditure within 3 years.) Write or phone. If, after a survey, we promise to reduce your factory heating bills next winter, and don't, we'll pay them.

Colt International Limited (Heating, Ventilation and Industrial Access) Havant, Hants. Telephone Havant 6411. Telex 86219.

If Colt can't reduce your factory heating bills this winter, they'll pay them.

Fig. 5.11 (courtesy Colt International Ltd)

Problems

Temperatures

1. Why are freezing and boiling points so useful as *fixed* points for the calibration of thermometers?
2. What would be reasonable temperatures for the following:
   (a) a cold winter's day,
   (b) a hot summer's day,
   (c) room temperature in your classroom?

Heat as energy

3. How would you convince a fellow student that heat is a form of energy and not some fluid which can be squeezed out of matter, being invisible and occupying the minute spaces between the atoms?
4. To heat a block of steel, mass 1 kg, so that its temperature rises by 1 deg C, 480 J of energy is needed. How much energy would be needed for a 3 kg block of steel? What assumption do you need to make to answer the question?
5. The specific heat capacity of water is 4200 J/kg/deg C.
   (a) How much energy is needed to raise the temperature of 500 g of water by 5 deg C?
   (b) What temperature change is produced when 8400 J of energy are supplied to 2 kg of water?
   Assume that all the supplied energy goes into heating the water.
6. One kilogramme of water is contained in an aluminium pan having a mass of 100 g. The specific heat capacity of water is 4200 J/kg/deg C, and that of aluminium is 920 J/kg/deg C.
   (a) How much energy is needed to raise the temperature of the pan by 50 deg C?
   (b) How much energy is needed to raise the temperature of the water by 50 deg C?
   (c) How much energy is needed to raise the temperature of the pan full of water by 50 deg C?
   (d) If in heating up the pan full of water only 50 per cent of the supplied energy actually heats the pan and water, the other 50 per cent being lost to the surroundings, how much energy is needed to raise the temperature of the pan full of water by 50 deg C?

Change of state

7. The specific latent heat of fusion of water is 334 000 J/kg.
   (a) How much energy is needed to melt a block of ice, at 0°C, having a mass of 500 g?
   (b) How much energy has to be removed from water at 0°C in order that it can freeze?
8. The specific latent heat of vaporization of water is 2 270 000 J/kg. How much energy is needed to evaporate 200 g of water at 100°C?

9. The specific heat capacity of water is 4200 J/kg/deg C; the specific latent heat of vaporization is 2 270 000 J/kg.
   (a) How much energy is needed to raise 500 g of water from 20°C to 100°C?
   (b) How much energy is needed to transform 500 g of liquid water to steam at 100°C?
   (c) How much energy is needed to change 500 g of water at 20°C to steam at 100°C?
10. The specific latent heat of fusion of copper is 206 000 J/kg at the normal melting point of 1084°C. How much energy is needed to change 50 kg of copper at 1084°C into liquid copper?
11. Figure 5.12 is a graph showing how the range of temperatures over which melting occurs for alloys of copper and nickel, depends on the relative percentages of the two components in the alloy. Estimate the percentages of nickel and copper in an alloy of the two that starts to melt at 1300°C and is completely liquid at 1365°C.

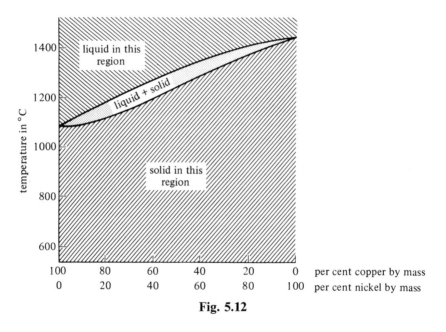

Fig. 5.12

The effects of heat

12. Explain how the joint in the railway lines allows expansion to occur, without resulting in a derailing of a train.
13. Thick glass tumblers are often broken when very hot water is poured into them. Why do you think this happens?
14. If two strips of different metals are fixed together (Fig. 5.13) and the strip is heated, what do you think will happen? The two metals expand by different amounts for the same temperature rise.

Figure 5.14 shows such a bimetallic strip in an electric iron. The strip is used as a thermostat, a means of controlling the temperature of the iron. Explain how it works.

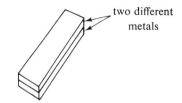

Fig. 5.13

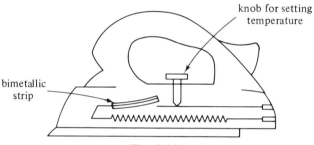

Fig. 5.14

15. Why do long lengths of hot-water pipes often have a loop in them; Fig. 5.15?
16. Design an experiment to show that different liquids expand by different amounts for the same temperature rise.
17. Explain how a hot-air balloon works.

Fig. 5.15

Transfer of heat
18. Lay your hand flat on a number of different surfaces in a room. All the objects will be at about the same temperature in the room, but some will conduct heat away from your hand better than others. Tabulate your findings in a list of good and bad conductors of heat.
19. When two similar size bars of copper and iron each have an end placed in a fire, it is observed that the end of the iron bar in the fire becomes red hot more rapidly than the corresponding end of the copper bar. Why? If you held the ends of the bars that were not in the fire what difference might you expect?

20. You can easily tell the difference between stepping, in your bare feet, onto lino tiles or onto carpet, one seems much colder than the other. Why?
21. Draw a diagram of a domestic hot water system and explain how the system works.
22. Why do clothes keep us warm?
23. How is the heat from a car engine dissipated in order to prevent the temperature of the engine rising too high?
24. Design an experiment to show that heat radiation travels in straight lines.

Thermal insulation
25. Boxes made of expanded polystyrene are used to contain objects, perhaps ice cream, which are wanted to be kept cold. Why is expanded polystyrene a good substance to use?

Discussion points

1. A considerable amount of fuel is wasted in both the domestic house and in factories because insufficient attention is paid to insulation. Consider your own home, or the place where you work, and the possible ways in which better insulation could conserve fuel. Against the cost of further insulation you have to balance the extra cost of the insulation, but there is also the point that the world's stock of fossil fuels is limited and that conservation is in the interests of mankind.
2. The efficiency of a modern power station is of the order of 35 to 40 per cent, the remaining 60 to 65 per cent being waste heat which has to be removed. This need to get rid of heat energy governs the location of power stations. Some power stations are alongside rivers or the sea, others have large cooling towers. The bigger the power station the greater the problem becomes of getting rid of the waste heat. As the years progress we use more and more energy, e.g., more electric machines in the home, more factories using machines to produce goods. What effect do you think this will have on the location of future power stations? Will there be problems of location in a crowded island such as Britain?

Background reading

Angrist, S. W., and L. G. Hepler, *Order and Chaos*, Penguin, 1973.
Chapters 2 and 3 are particularly relevant, chapter 2 concerning temperature, and chapter 3 the conservation of energy and the idea of heat as a form of energy.

6. Electricity

6.1 The electric circuit

Given a torch battery, a torch bulb, and wire, how would you arrange the items so that the bulb lights? Figure 6.1(a) shows how it can be done. Figure 6.1(b) shows how items such as a battery, bulb, and connecting wire can be represented in a circuit diagram. For the bulb to light there must be

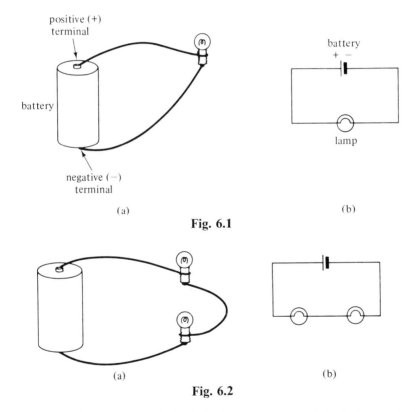

(a)

(b)

Fig. 6.1

(a)

(b)

Fig. 6.2

a connection from one terminal of the battery to one of the bulb terminals and then a connection from the other terminal of the bulb to the other battery terminal. We say there has to be a complete circuit.

If we connect another bulb into our circuit (Fig. 6.2), and arrange the connections so that the wires go from a battery to one bulb, then the other, and then finally back to the battery, we find that both bulbs, assuming they are the same type of bulb, light with equal brightness. This type of connection is called a *series* connection. If we connect three such bulbs in series (Fig. 6.3), then each of the bulbs has the same brightness, but the more bulbs we put in the series circuit the less bright any one bulb becomes.

Circuit	*Brightness of bulbs*
one bulb	bright
two bulbs in series	not so bright
three bulbs in series	very dim

If one of the bulbs in our three-in-series circuit were to break, then all of the bulbs would cease to light. One bulb defective means that there is a break in the circuit.

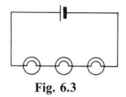

Fig. 6.3

If one of the bulbs in your home burns out all the bulbs do not go out. A series form of circuit thus cannot be the type of circuit used in a house wiring installation. The type of circuit used has *parallel* connections. Figure 6.4 shows how the three bulbs can be connected in parallel. If one of the bulbs is removed the other two remain alight. Taking out a bulb does not

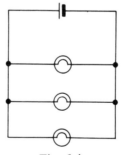

Fig. 6.4

break the circuit to the other bulbs; there is still a continuity of connection from one terminal of the battery through a lamp and back to the other battery terminal.

This need for a continuity of circuit from one terminal of the battery through the lamp and then back to the other battery terminal suggests that perhaps something is flowing round the circuit and that in order to flow it must have a completed path. We talk of there being a *current* in the circuit.

We can tell when a current is flowing because a bulb will light. With no current there is no lighting of the bulb.

6.2 Ammeters and voltmeters

When three bulbs are connected in series, as in Fig. 6.3, the lamps are equally bright, so that, provided we can consider brightness to be some measure of current, the current is the same at all points in such a circuit. If we put an instrument called an *ammeter* in the series circuit it does not matter where we put the meter, as long as it is in series, the same reading is obtained. Also, if the brightness of the bulbs increases the reading on the ammeter increases. Thus, if we put the meter in the series circuit having just two bulbs the ammeter reading is higher. The instrument thus can be considered to give us a measure of the current in the circuit.

The reading given by an ammeter is in units called amperes (A). Common prefixes used with the unit are milli-amperes (mA) for one thousandth of an ampere, and micro-ampere (μA) for one millionth of an ampere.

There is another instrument in common use with electrical circuits, it is called a *voltmeter*. If we take our circuit with three bulbs and one battery in series, the bulbs light only very dimly. If, however, we use two batteries, connected as shown in Fig. 6.5, then the lamps are much brighter. With

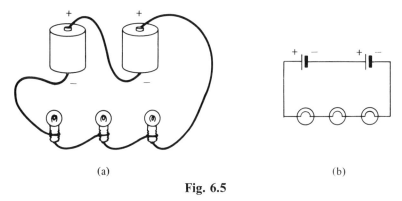

(a)   (b)

Fig. 6.5

three batteries the lamps are brighter still. Increasing the number of batteries has increased the brightness of the lamps. If we connect the voltmeter in parallel with one battery we might obtain a reading of 1·5 V; across the two batteries the reading would be 3·0 V and across the three, 4·5 V. The voltmeter might thus be considered to give some sort of measure of battery strength, in volts.

When a lamp is glowing there is energy being dissipated. The bulb is hot. This energy is supplied by the battery. If the brightness of a lamp is increased then the energy supplied must be increased. When the energy supply is increased the voltmeter reading increases. The voltmeter might thus be considered as a measure of the energy supply.

An important point to remember is that: ammeters are always connected in series with the component through which you want to determine the current, voltmeters are connected in parallel with the component across which you wish to measure the voltage.

There is another point of importance. When two batteries are connected in series and a voltmeter is connected across the two, then the voltage might be zero. If the terminal labelled with a negative sign on the first battery is connected to the negative terminal of the second battery (Fig. 6.6(a)) and then the voltmeter is connected to the two terminals labelled with positive signs, then the result can be zero. For the voltages of the two batteries to add up the positive terminal of one battery has to be connected to the negative terminal of the other, and the voltmeter must be connected between the other positive and negative terminals; Fig. 6.6(b).

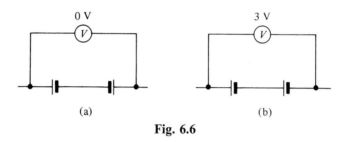

Fig. 6.6

6.3 Potential difference

You might consider that the quantity measured by a voltmeter was the voltage, there is, however, another term used to describe the quantity measured by a voltmeter—*potential difference*. When a voltmeter is connected between two points it is said to be measuring the potential difference between those points. This is a measure of the energy dissipated in the current passing through the component concerned.

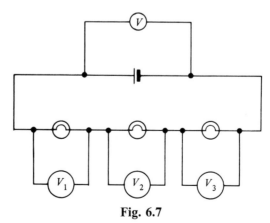

Fig. 6.7

If we put a voltmeter across each of the components in a series circuit (Fig. 6.7), then the potential difference across the battery is equal to the sum of the potential differences across each of the components:

$$V = V_1 + V_2 + V_3$$

6.4 Resistance

Suppose we assemble a circuit with an ammeter in series with a component, perhaps a lamp, and a voltmeter in parallel with it, the source of the voltage being a battery; Fig. 6.8. We can then read the potential difference, V, and

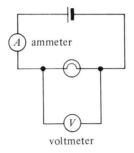

voltmeter

Fig. 6.8

the current, I, from the meters. Suppose the result was 1·5 V and 0·3 A. Another component might give us the readings 1·5 V and 0·5 A. For the same potential difference the second component allows more current to pass. We say that it has less *resistance*. Resistance is defined as the ratio of the potential difference and the current.

$$\text{resistance} = \frac{\text{potential difference}}{\text{current}}$$

or, using the conventional symbols,

$$R = \frac{V}{I}$$

When the unit of potential difference is the volt and that of the current the ampere, then the unit of resistance is the ohm (symbol Ω). Hence, for the two components already referred to, we have:

$$R = \frac{V}{I} = \frac{1 \cdot 5}{0 \cdot 3} = 5\,\Omega$$

$$R = \frac{V}{I} = \frac{1 \cdot 5}{0 \cdot 5} = 3\,\Omega$$

The second component, that allowed *more* current to pass round the circuit for the *same* potential difference, has a *lower* resistance than the first component.

87

A lamp bulb is just a small coil of wire, or perhaps just a single loop, in a sealed bulb. We can measure the potential difference across, and the current through, a length of wire without having it in a bulb. For a 1 metre length of constantan wire (diameter 0·274 mm, termed 32 standard wire gauge or 32 s.w.g.) a potential difference of 1·6 V was found to occur with a current of 0·2 A. The resistance is, therefore,

$$R = \frac{V}{I} = \frac{1\cdot6}{0\cdot2} = 8\ \Omega$$

With a 2 m length of the same wire the potential difference was 1·6 V for a current of 0·1 A. The resistance is thus

$$R = \frac{V}{I} = \frac{1\cdot6}{0\cdot1} = 16\ \Omega$$

The resistance of the wire obviously depends on the length of the wire. Double the length means double the resistance.

We can take a 1 m length of constantan wire and measure the current through it for different potential differences, perhaps using one, then two, etc., batteries in the circuit shown in Fig. 6.8. Typical results for such an experiment are:

Potential difference in volts	Current in amperes	$R (= V/I)$
0	0	—
1·6	0·2	8
3·2	0·4	8
4·8	0·6	8

The resistance seems to be independent of the current. If we plot a graph of potential difference against current (Fig. 6.9) the graph is a straight line, showing that the current is proportional to the potential difference. This relationship is known as *Ohm's law*.

Not all materials obey Ohm's law. Figure 6.10 shows the potential difference–current graph for a torch bulb. Only for small currents is the graph a possible approximation to a straight line.

If we know that for a 2 m length of constantan wire the potential difference of 1·6 V gives a current of 0·1 A, then the resistance at that current is 16 Ω. If we assume that Ohm's law is obeyed we can calculate what the potential difference must be for a current of 0·4 A.

$$R = \frac{V}{I} = \frac{V}{0\cdot4} = 8$$

Hence

$$V = 3\cdot2\ \text{V}$$

88

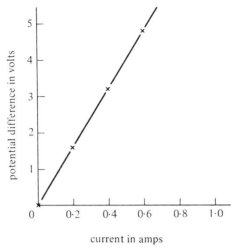

current in amps

Fig. 6.9

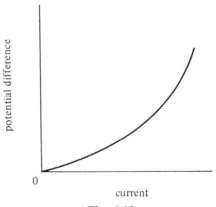

current

Fig. 6.10

6.5 Series and parallel resistors

A *resistor* is an electrical component which is used, in a circuit, to provide a certain resistance. In the circuit shown in Fig. 6.11 the circuit symbol for a resistor is shown. If we have a number of resistors in series, what is the total resistance of the combination? If we have a number of resistors in parallel what is the total resistance of the combination?

For resistors in series we must have the same current flowing through each resistor. It does not matter which side of a resistor we put an ammeter, the current is the same. We also must have the potential differences across each resistor adding up to give the total potential difference across the entire series group of resistors. If we have potential difference of 1 V across the first resistor, 2 V across the second, and 3 V across the third, then the total potential difference across the three resistors must be $1+2+3 = 6$ V. If we replaced the three resistors by a single resistor having the same effect on the circuit, then the potential difference across it would have to be 6 V. If the current through each resistor was 0·2 A, then the current through the replacement single resistor would have to be 0·2 A. Hence, the value of this resistor must be $6/0·2 = 30\ \Omega$.

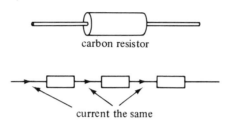

carbon resistor

current the same

resistors in series

Fig. 6.11

The above argument can be presented algebraically. If the potential differences across each of the three resistors is V_1, V_2, V_3 then the potential difference across the single replacement resistor must be

$$V = V_1 + V_2 + V_3$$

If we divide both sides of the equation by the current, I, then

$$\frac{V}{I} = \frac{V_1}{I} + \frac{V_2}{I} + \frac{V_3}{I}$$

But $V_1/I = R_1$, $V_2/I = R_2$, $V_3/I = R_3$ and V/I is the value of the resistance of the replacement resistor; the current is the same for each resistor. Hence

$$R = R_1 + R_2 + R_3$$

To find the total resistance of resistors in series just add the separate resistances.

For resistors in parallel (Fig. 6.12) we have the following experimental facts: a voltmeter placed across each resistor shows the same potential difference for each of the resistors; ammeters placed in series with the resistors show that the current entering a circuit junction equals the current leaving the junction. Thus, we might have a potential difference across each resistor of 3 V. If we replace the three resistors by a single resistor, and we want the effect on the circuit to be unchanged, then the potential difference across this single replacement resistor must be 3 V. If the current through the first resistor is 0·1 A, that through the second resistor 0·2 A, and that through the third 0·3 A, then the total current entering the parallel arrangement must be

$$0·1 + 0·2 + 0·3 = 0·6\ \text{A}$$

Hence, the current through the single replacement resistor must be 0·6 A. It's resistance must be $3/0·6 = 5\ \Omega$.

The above argument can be presented algebraically. If the potential difference across each resistor is V then the potential difference across the replacement resistor must be V. If the current through the resistors is I_1, I_2, I_3 then the current through the replacement resistor must be

$$I = I_1 + I_2 + I_3$$

Dividing both sides of the equation by V gives

$$\frac{I}{V} = \frac{I_1}{V} + \frac{I_2}{V} + \frac{I_3}{V}$$

But $I_1/V = 1/R_2$, $I_2/V = 1/R_2$, $I_3/V = 1/R_3$ and I/V is the value of the reciprocal of resistance of the replacement resistor. Hence

$$\frac{1}{R} = \frac{1}{R_1} + \frac{1}{R_2} + \frac{1}{R_3}$$

We have to use reciprocals to find the value of the resistance of a parallel set of resistors.

this voltmeter is
across each resistor

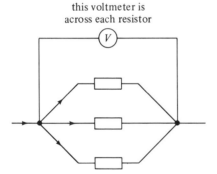
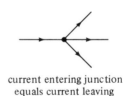

current entering junction
equals current leaving

Fig. 6.12

What is the resistance of 3 Ω and 6 Ω in series? The total resistance is $3 + 6 = 9\ \Omega$. What is the total resistance if the 3 Ω and 6 Ω resistors are placed in parallel?

$$\frac{1}{R} = \frac{1}{3} + \frac{1}{6}$$

$$\frac{1}{R} = \frac{2+1}{6}$$

Hence

$$R = 2\ \Omega$$

91

6.6 Resistivity

One metre of constantan wire with a diameter of 0·274 mm (32 s.w.g.) has a resistance of 8 Ω. Two metres of the same wire has a resistance of 16 Ω, 3 m a resistance of 24 Ω. Doubling the length doubles the resistance. Trebling the length trebles the resistance. The resistance is proportional to the length of the wire.

One metre of constantan wire with a diameter of 0·559 mm (24 s.w.g.) has a resistance of 2 Ω. This diameter is about double that of the 8 Ω per metre constantan wire. Double the diameter means the resistance decreasing by a factor of four. Because the cross-sectional area of the wire is proportional to the square of the diameter, doubling the diameter has increased the area by a factor of four. Thus increasing the area by a factor of four has resulted in the resistance decreasing by a factor of four. The resistance is inversely proportional to the area.

We can summarize these two relationships as

$$\text{resistance } R \propto \text{length } L$$

$$\text{resistance } R \propto \frac{1}{\text{area } A}$$

Combining these two relationships gives:

$$\text{resistance } R \propto \frac{L}{A}$$

If we increase the area by a factor of four we must increase the length by a factor of four to keep the resistance the same, i.e., L/A constant. A 4 m length of constantan wire of 0·274 mm diameter has a resistance equal to that of 1 metre of constantan wire of diameter 0·559 mm.

Copper wire of diameter 0·274 mm (32 s.w.g.) has a resistance of 0·3 Ω per metre. The resistance thus depends on what the nature of the material is, in this case whether it is copper or constantan. We define a quantity called resistivity ρ to take account of the nature of the material.

$$R = \rho \frac{L}{A}$$

The unit of resistivity is ohm metre (Ω m).

Constantan has a resistivity of about 0·50 μΩ m, i.e., $0·50 \times 10^{-6}$ Ω m, copper has a resistivity of about 0·02 μΩ m, about 1/25 that of constantan. The resistance of 1 metre of copper wire of diameter 0·274 mm is about 1/25 that of constantan wire of the same length and diameter.

The following are the resistivities of typical materials, at room temperature.

Material	Resistivity in ohm metres	
aluminium	$2·5 \times 10^{-8}$	
copper	$1·7 \times 10^{-8}$	good conductors
iron	$10·0 \times 10^{-8}$	

Material	Resistivity in ohm metres	
germanium	0·009	semi-conductors
silicon	10·0	
glass	10^{10}	insulators
dry paper	10^{10}	
PVC	10^{12}	

Good conductors of electricity have very low resistivities, of the order of a millionth of an ohm metre. Insulators have very high resistivities, of the order of millions of millions of ohm metres. Semiconductors have, as their name might imply, resistivities between the two extremes of good and bad conductors.

A strip of material with a cubic shape, and having a side of the cube equal to 1 mm, has a cross-sectional area of 1 mm². This is 10^{-6} m², i.e., a millionth of a square metre. A 1 m length of such a strip would, if made of copper, have a resistance

$$R = \rho \frac{L}{A} = \frac{1·7 \times 10^{-8} \times 1}{10^{-6}} = 0·017 \ \Omega$$

If the strip was made of silicon it would have a resistance

$$R = \rho \frac{L}{A} = \frac{10 \times 1}{10^{-6}} = 10^7 \ \Omega$$

If the strip was glass the resistance would be

$$R = \rho \frac{L}{A} = \frac{10^{10} \times 1}{10^{-6}} = 10^{16} \ \Omega$$

Electrical connecting wires are generally made of copper wire covered by a layer of a plastic such as PVC. The copper has a low resistivity and so offers little resistance to a current; the PVC has a very high resistivity and so offers a very very high resistance to a current. The result of this is that the current essentially flows along the wire and not through the plastic.

In electronic circuits resistors made of small pieces of carbon are common. Carbon has a resistivity of about 60 Ω m. Thus a small rod of carbon can be used to give a resistance of, say, a thousand ohms.

6.7 Circuits with a battery

Suppose we connect a battery in series with an ammeter and a variable resistor, connecting a voltmeter in parallel with the battery; Fig. 6.13. The variable resistor may be in the form of a coil of wire over which we can move a sliding contact. This varies the amount of resistance wire in the circuit. The graph in Fig. 6.13 shows how the ammeter and voltmeter readings change as the circuit resistance is changed. The voltage drops as the current taken from the battery increases.

We can extrapolate the graph back to what the voltage would be if we took zero current from the battery. The value of this voltage, when the current taken is zero, is called the electro-motive-force (e.m.f.) of the battery.

The graph in Fig. 6.13 shows an e.m.f. of 1·5 V. At a current of 0·2 A the voltmeter reading is 1·3 V. What has happened to the difference between the 1·3 and 1·5 V, i.e., the missing 0·2 V? This difference can be explained by considering the battery to have an internal resistance. The e.m.f. has to drive the current through both the internal resistance and the external resistor.

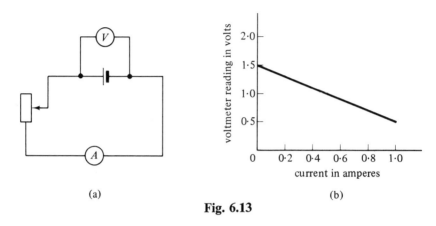

(a)   (b)

Fig. 6.13

The internal and external resistors are considered to be in series and so the potential difference of 1·5 V is across both resistors. The voltmeter reads the part of the potential difference across the external resistor, i.e., 1·3 V. Hence, there is a potential difference of 0·2 V across the internal resistor. At a current of 0·2 A this means a resistance of 1 Ω.

$$R = \frac{V}{I} = \frac{0·2}{0·2} = 1\ \Omega$$

Knowing this internal resistance, we can calculate what the potential difference applied to the circuit would be if we take a current of say 0·5 A.

$$R = 1 = \frac{V}{0·5}$$

Hence the potential difference across the internal resistance would be 0·5 V, and the potential difference available would be 1·5 − 0·5 = 1·0 V.

6.8 The effects of currents

When a current passes through the wire in a lamp bulb, the wire becomes hot. When a current passes through any wire its temperature increases, the amount of the increase depending on the size of the current and the resistance of the wire concerned. This heating effect of a current has obvious uses in items such as an electric fire, the heating element of an electric kettle, or a soldering iron; Fig. 6.14(a).

When a current is passed through a wire a magnetic effect is produced. You may be familiar with the conventional bar or horseshoe magnet. If you sprinkle iron filings near such a magnet they become attracted to the magnet. if a compass needle is placed near a magnet it is also affected. A current

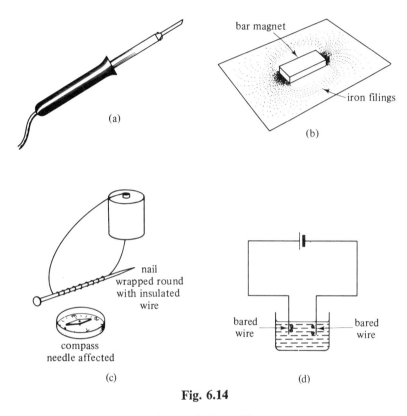

Fig. 6.14

passing through a wire makes it behave like a magnet, attracting iron filings and affecting a compass needle; Fig. 6.14(b). A coil of wire wrapped round a piece of soft iron, not itself a magnet, can be quite a strong magnet when a current is passed through the wire. Such a magnet is called an *electromagnet*. A simple arrangement for an electromagnet is shown in Fig. 6.14(c), together with its effect on a compass needle.

Some liquids are good conductors of electricity. Figure 6.14(c) shows the type of arrangement by which the resistance between two electrical contacts immersed in a liquid can be measured. The electrical contacts are called *electrodes*, and a solution which conducts well is called an *electrolyte*. If you did the experiment with two electrodes dipping into tap water, gases might be seen bubbling off at the two electrodes. If copper sulphate is used then one of the electrodes becomes coated with copper. Passing a current through such liquids gives rise to chemical effects (chapter 8 looks more closely at these effects).

6.9 Power

When a current passes through a wire it becomes hot. Indeed in some cases the wire may become so hot that it melts. Such an effect is useful in the case of a fuse. Such a component is inserted into a circuit and melts when the current rises too high. The fuse is generally a small piece of wire. When the wire melts it breaks the circuit, and so stops high currents burning out equipment.

Energy is being dissipated when a current passes through a wire—energy in the form of heat. An immersion heater used to heat the water in the hot water supply of a house is only a coil of wire which gets hot when a current passes through it. But why does only the coil part of the electric circuit become appreciably hot, why does the entire circuit not become hot? Why in the case of a fuse is it only that part of the circuit that gets so hot that it melts?

Suppose we put an immersion heater in a hole in a block of aluminium (Fig. 6.15) and a thermometer into another hole in the block. We then measure the current passing through the heater, and the voltage across the

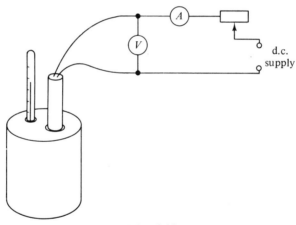

Fig. 6.15

heater. The thermometer enables us to determine how the temperature rise in the block of aluminium is related to changes in the electrical current and potential difference. If we double the current and the potential difference also doubles we find that the temperature rise per second, or minute or some convenient time interval, increase by a factor of four. If both the current and the potential difference are trebled, then the temperature rise per second increases by a factor of nine. The inference is that the energy dissipated per second is proportional to the product of the current and the potential difference. The energy dissipated per second is called the *power*. The equation relating the power, and the current, and potential difference, is taken as

$$\text{power} = IV$$

If the current is in amperes and the potential difference in volts, then the power is in watts.

As $V = IR$ we can rearrange the power equation to give

$$\text{power} = I \times IR = I^2 R$$

The reason why the fuse wire melts, and not the rest of the circuit, is that the fuse wire is a thin piece of resistance wire and thin pieces of wire have higher resistances than thick pieces. The fuse wire has a higher resistance than the connecting wires. The immersion heater coil has a higher resistance than the other wires in the circuit. To dissipate a lot of energy we need high resistance and a large current.

An electric fire element has a power of 1 kW when connected to the mains electric supply. This means that every second, 1000 J of energy are being dissipated; 1 W is 1 J per second. If the electric fire is left switched on for 1 min, 60 s, then the energy dissipated is 60×1000 J.

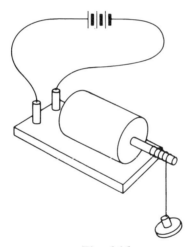

Fig. 6.16

You may feel that there is no link between electrical power and the term power you meet with in terms of the rate of doing mechanical work. We could measure, however, the energy produced by passing a current through a resistance, by taking as the resistance coil, the coil in an electric motor. When we pass a current through the coil in the electric motor then the motor axle rotates and this can be used to wind up a load; Fig. 6.16. The rate at which the load is lifted, i.e., the rate at which mechanical work is done, can be measured and compared with values of the current and potential difference for the electric circuit. The power is still given by power $= IV$.

97

The following are typical power ratings of some appliances you may have in your home. The actual power used will depend on the circumstances, e.g., volume or brightness setting.

Electric fire element	1 kW
Electric iron	700 W
Television receiver	150 W
Tape recorder	50 W

The bill you pay for your electricity is in terms of the energy you use. The charge is reckoned in terms of the number of kilowatt hours used. One kilowatt hour is the energy used when 1 kW is being dissipated for an entire hour. Thus, the 1 kW electric fire element uses 1 kW h of electricity if left on for 1 h. If left on for 5 h then the energy used is 5 kW h. The tape recorder has to be left on for 20 h to use 1 kW h of electricity. One kilowatt hour is 1000 W for 3600 s, and so is 3600 000 J of energy.

For the connection of an appliance, such as the electric fire, to the mains supply it is common practice to use electric plugs that have a fuse fixed

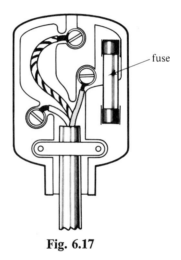

Fig. 6.17

inside them; Fig. 6.17. The fuse is in the form of a small glass tube in which the fine wire is situated. When the current in the circuit rises too high the wire burns out. For the 1 kW electric fire on the 240 V mains supply the current will be given by

$$\text{power} = 1000 = I \times 240$$

Hence

$$I = 4 \cdot 2 \text{ A}$$

The fuse used with such an appliance would thus be the nearest standard value above 4·2 A, i.e., a fuse marked as 5 A. Thus, provided the current remains at the normal value for the fire, the fuse will not burn out. If the current rises significantly above the normal running current then the fuse burns out.

The current taken by the television receiver, 150 W, is given by

$$power = 150 = I \times 240$$

Hence

$$I = 0.63 \text{ A}$$

The standard fuse to fit in the plug for the television receiver is 2 A.

The plug shown in Fig. 6.17 has three pins. To make the electric fire work only two of the pins are needed. In making a torch bulb light you need only two connections, one from each side of the battery. To make the electric fire work you just need two connections, one from each side of the mains supply, termed the live and neutral (as opposed to positive and negative for a battery). The third connection, however, has an important function. It is called the *earth* connection. The earth lead is connected at one end to the metal frame of the electric fire and at the other end to the earth, a metal plate buried in the ground. If the live wire to the fire became loose and touched the frame of the fire there is a low resistance path via the earth wire to earth. If you touched the frame of the fire you would offer a higher resistance path to the earth, and so a greater current would pass along the lower resistance earth wire than through you. The current passes to the earth because back at the substation of the electricity board they have connected the neutral wire to earth. The complete circuit consists of the live terminal at the substation connected to the fire element, then via the loose connection to the fire frame, then via the earth lead back to the neutral terminal at the substation. The purpose of the earth connection is to make appliances safer.

The equation power $= IV$ really applies only to circuits involving just resistors, the presence of other circuit elements modifies the equation.

6.10 Electromagnetism

When a current passes through a wire a magnetic field is produced. We can detect the magnetic field by the action of the field on a magnet. A magnet, perhaps a compass needle, experiences a force when in a magnetic field. The Earth has a magnetic field and so a compass needle, set in the field, experiences forces which rotate the needle until it lines up with the field, pointing north and south. But a current passing through a wire seems to make it behave like a magnet, so should we not expect that a current-carrying wire placed in a magnetic field would experience a force. It does. Figure 6.18 shows a simple arrangement by which this can be shown. The apparatus is called a current balance. When a current passes through the balance wire, it moves in the magnetic field. The balance can be restored to its equilibrium position by putting weight on the balance wire—in fact, we are weighing the current. Our unit of current, the ampere, is defined in terms of the force acting on a current-carrying wire, when placed in a magnetic field produced by a current in another wire. We can thus establish the scale on an ammeter by using a current balance. This is the basis of the International standard of current.

A current passing through a wire in a magnetic field experiences a force. The direction of the force is at right-angles both to the current in the wire and to the direction of the magnetic field; Fig. 6.19. You may already have come across applications of this effect—ammeters and motors. Figure 6.19(a) shows the basic design of a meter, and Fig. 6.19(c) that of a motor. In both cases there is a coil through which current is passed and, as the coil is in a magnetic field, a force acts on it. The directions of the magnetic field and the wires are such that the forces acting on the coil cause it to rotate. In the case of the meter the coil rotates against a spring, rotating until the forces acting on the coil are balanced by the opposing forces produced by squashing the

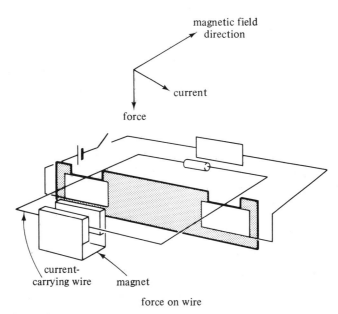

Fig. 6.18   (from *Patterns in Physics*, W. Bolton, McGraw-Hill, 1974)

spring. The rotation is shown by a pointer attached to the coil. In the case of the motor there is no spring, and the coil is allowed to rotate. To keep the coil rotating in the same direction the current to the coil has to be reversed every half-rotation.

A current in a wire produces a magnetic field. Can we produce a current by the use of a magnetic field? The answer is yes. If a magnet is moved near a wire connected to the terminals of a meter, then a current reading will show on the meter as long as there is relative movement of the magnetic field to the wire. When there is no movement then there is no current produced; Fig. 6.20. This effect is called *electromagnetic induction*.

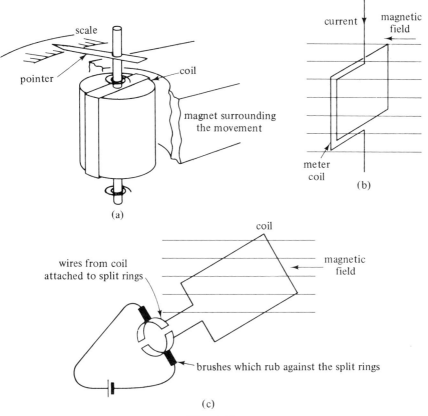

scale

pointer

coil

magnet surrounding
the movement

(a)

current

magnetic
field

meter
coil

(b)

coil

wires from coil
attached to split rings

magnetic
field

brushes which rub against the split rings

(c)

Fig. 6.19

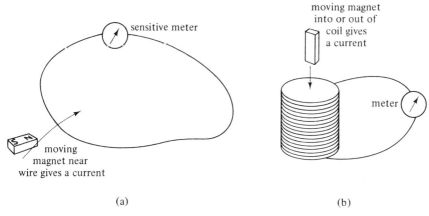

sensitive meter

moving
magnet near
wire gives a current

(a)

moving magnet
into or out of
coil gives
a current

meter

(b)

Fig. 6.20

If a bar magnet is moved backwards and forwards into a coil of wire connected to a meter then an alternating current is produced; Fig. 6.21. When one pole of the magnet moves into the coil the current goes in one direction, when the pole moves out the current flows in the other direction. We can have the coil moving and the magnet stationary and still get the same effect. Figure 6.22 shows such an effect being used as the basis of an alternating current generator. The coil rotates in a magnetic field and has currents produced in it which can be fed to external electrical circuits. The mains supply in your home, or factory, or college, is an alternating current supply, produced in a manner comparable to that shown by Fig. 6.22.

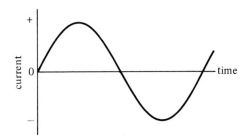

current variation with time produced
by the mains supply, the magnet moving
into and out of the coil approximates crudely
to this

Fig. 6.21

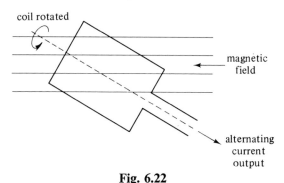

Fig. 6.22

6.11 Electrostatics

If you rub a piece of plastic, perhaps the cover of a pen, against wool the plastic, when put near small pieces of paper, picks up the paper. We say that the plastic has been charged by the rubbing with wool. Many materials when rubbed together become charged. It is not only the plastic that is charged but also the wool with which it was rubbed. If we rub two strips of the same plastic against the same piece of wool and then suspend or pivot one of them so that it is free to move, we find that on bringing up to it the other charged piece of plastic that the two repel each other; Fig. 6.23. *Like charges repel.* If we bring up to the suspended charged piece of plastic the piece of wool then we find that the wool attracts the plastic. We can give an explanation of this in terms of both the wool and plastic being initially uncharged. On rubbing together, charge moves from one to the other, leaving one with a surplus of charge and the other with a deficiency. The one with the surplus we call negatively charged, the one with a deficiency positively charged. A positively charged object attracts a negatively charged object, *unlike charges attract.*

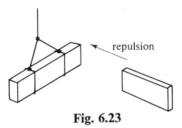

Fig. 6.23

The negative charge carriers that move in such a process are given a name—*electrons.*

If we have two objects one having positive charge, and the other negative, and then connect them by a copper wire, the charges appear to cancel each other. If we connect a meter by wires to the two objects then a current appears when the charges are cancelling each other out. A current appears to involve a movement of charge.

Problems

The electric circuit

1. In which of the circuits shown in Fig. 6.24 will the electric bulbs light?

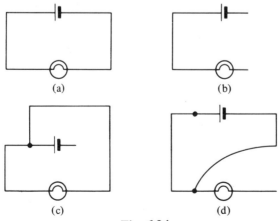

Fig. 6.24

103

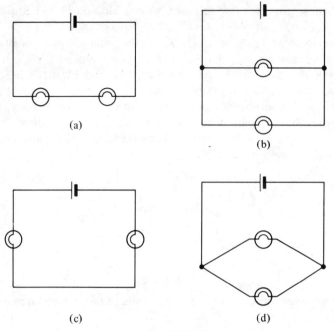

(a)

(b)

(c)

(d)

Fig. 6.25

2. In which of the circuits in Fig. 6.25 will removing one bulb make the other bulbs go out?

Ammeters and voltmeters

3. Which of the marked meter positions in Fig. 6.26 would be the ammeter and which the voltmeter, for a measurement of the current through the lamp and the voltage supplied by the battery?

4. Draw a diagram showing how you would connect three torch batteries so that their voltages added up to give the maximum voltage possible.

Potential difference

5. What would be the readings of the unlabelled voltmeters in Fig. 6.27?

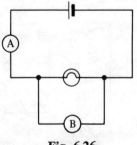

A

B

Fig. 6.26

Resistance

6. The potential difference across a resistor is 4·0 V and the current passing through it is 0·1 A. What is its resistance?
7. What is the current that will pass through a resistor of 10 Ω, if the potential difference across it is 1·5 V?
8. What is the potential difference across a resistor of 50 Ω when the current through it is 0·2 A?
9. The potential difference across a resistor is 2·0 V when the current through it is 0·1 A. If Ohm's law applies to the resistor, what will be the potential difference across it when the current is 0·3 A?
10. The following are experimental results of measurements of the potential difference across a resistor and the current through it.

Potential difference in volts	0	1·2	3·0	4·1	5·3	6·3	7·5
Current in amperes	0	0·25	0·60	0·82	1·10	1·25	1·50

   (a) Plot a graph of potential difference against current.
   (b) Does the resistor obey Ohm's law?
   (c) What is the resistance at currents of (i) 0·60 A, (ii) 1·25 A?

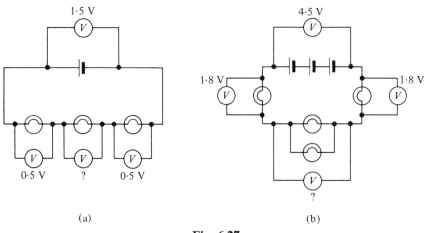

(a)

(b)

Fig. 6.27

11. The following are experimental results of measurements of the potential difference across a lamp and the current passed by the lamp,

Potential difference in volts	0	0·5	1·0	2·0	4·0	6·5	10·0
Current in amperes	0	0·50	0·90	1·30	1·70	2·30	2·80

   (a) Plot a graph of potential difference against current.
   (b) Does the lamp obey Ohm's law?
   (c) What is the resistance of the lamp at a current of (i) 0·50 A, (ii) 2·30 A?

Series and parallel resistors

12. What would be the equivalent resistor in the following cases?
    (a) 2 Ω and 3 Ω in series.
    (b) 12 Ω and 15 Ω in series.
    (c) 100 Ω, 150 Ω, and 300 Ω in series.
    (d) 5 Ω, 10 Ω, and 2 Ω in series.
    (e) 2 Ω and 2 Ω in parallel.
    (f) 4 Ω and 2 Ω in parallel.
    (g) 100 Ω and 400 Ω in parallel.
    (h) 2 Ω in parallel with 2 Ω in parallel with 2 Ω.
    (i) 4 Ω in parallel with 2 Ω in parallel with 10 Ω.

13. What must be the voltage and current readings on the unlabelled instruments in Fig. 6.28?

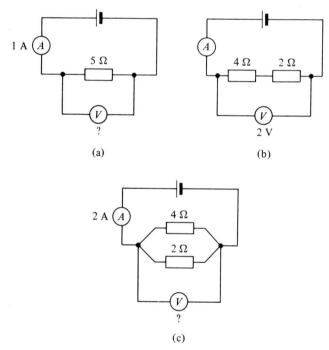

Fig. 6.28

Resistivity

14. Manganin wire of diameter 0·914 mm (20 s.w.g.) has a resistance per metre of 0·630 Ω. What would be the resistance per metre of manganin wire of diameter 0·457 mm (26 s.w.g.)?

15. Copper wire of diameter 2·0 mm has a resistance per metre of 0·0053 Ω. What would be the resistance of (a) 3 m, (b) 1 km of the wire?

106

16. Constantan has a resistivity of $0.50\ \mu\Omega$ m. Calculate the resistance of a 1 m length of constantan wire with a cross-sectional area of 1.5×10^{-6} m².

17. Carbon resistors are quite common in electronic circuits. Examine such a resistor and, from the value of the resistance given for the resistor and its dimensions, estimate the resistivity of carbon.

18. Why are the connecting wires in circuits usually made of copper wire?

Circuits with a battery

19. What would be the potential difference between the terminals of a battery of internal resistance $0.5\ \Omega$ and e.m.f. 1.5 V when the external circuit takes (a) 0.1 A, (b) 1.0 A from the battery?

20. A torch battery of internal resistance $1.0\ \Omega$ has an e.m.f. of 3.0 V. What is the potential difference across a torch bulb connected to the battery and which draws a current of 0.25 A?

The effects of currents

21. How would you make an electromagnet?

22. Figure 6.29 shows the results of students winding coils to make electro-magnets. Which electromagnet would be expected to be the best at picking up pieces of iron?

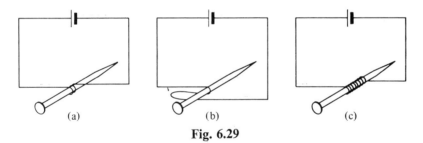

(a)   (b)   (c)

Fig. 6.29

Power

23. A torch bulb takes a current of 0.25 A for a potential difference of 1.5 V. What is the power of the bulb?

24. What is the energy dissipated, in joules, by a 2 kW electric fire in (a) 1 min, (b) 1 h?

25. What is the power dissipated when a current of 2 A flows through a resistance of $10\ \Omega$?

26. What is the function of a fuse in a circuit?

27. What is the current in a 60 W lamp when connected to 240 V?

28. What fuses should be fitted to the following apparatus when connected to a 240 V supply? Fuses of 2 A, 5 A, 10 A, and 13 A are available.
    (a) A 3 kW electric fire.
    (b) A refrigerator of 120 W.
    (c) A table lamp of 60 W.

29. How many kilowatt hours of electricity are used by
    (a) a 2 kW fire running for 6 h,
    (b) six lamps each of 100 W running for 4 h,
    (c) a television receiver of 150 W running for 6 h per day for an entire week.

Electromagnetism

30. Describe to a fellow student, who missed the appropriate lessons, how the following work:
    (a) the moving coil meter,
    (b) the d.c. motor.

Discussion points

Every house, every factory, in a technologically developed country, uses electricity. This is a characteristic of 20th-century life. How has the widespread use of electricity changed our lives? What was life like before electricity became used in this widespread way? What might life be like if we did not have this widespread use of electricity?

Background reading

Lewis, J. L., and Heafford, P. E., 'Electric currents', *Physics Topics*, Longman, 1969.

7. Waves

7.1 What are waves?

Figure 7.1 is a photograph of waves. The waves involve water moving. Figure 7.2 is a sketch of a wave travelling along a rope. The wave involves movement of parts of the rope. What is a wave? What have the water and

Fig. 7.1 Waves breaking on a shore (Aerofilms Ltd)

Fig. 7.2

rope in common which leads us to call the motion a wave motion? Something wags up-and-down or to-and-fro. If we watched a cork floating on the water surface we would see it bob up-and-down as the wave passed it. If we

109

watched a piece of thread tied to the rope we would see it move up-and-down as the wave passed.

If we had a whole line of corks floating on the water surface then, when a wave reached the first cork, that cork would bob up-and-down; Fig. 7.3. Then the wave would reach the second cork and cause that to bob up-and-down. Then the wave would reach the third cork and that would bob up-and-down, and so on down the line of corks. If the wave was a continuous wave we might have, at some instant of time, the first cork up at the crest of the wave, the second cork down in the trough, the third cork up at a crest, the fourth down in a trough, etc. At some later instant of time the situation might be that the first cork was down in a trough, the second cork at a crest, the third in a trough, the fourth at a crest, and so on; Fig. 7.3(e). Each cork moves up-and-down. The agent responsible for the up-and-down movement itself moves—the agent is called the wave.

The term *wavelength* is used to describe the distance between successive crests, or the distance between successive troughs; Fig. 7.4. Thus if the wavelength of the water waves in Fig. 7.1 was 2 m, then the distance between successive crests would be 2 m; the distance between successive troughs would also be 2 m.

If we observed one of the corks we could count how many times, in a second, it bobbed up-down-and-so-back-to-the-starting-point-again. This is called the *frequency*. Thus, if the frequency of the water waves were 4 per

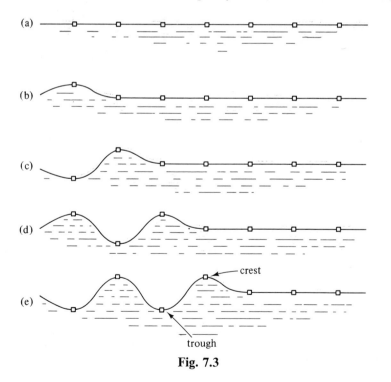

Fig. 7.3

110

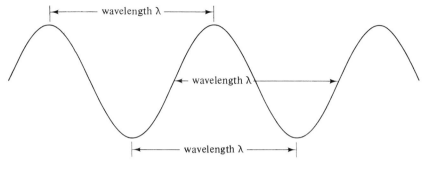

Fig. 7.4

second then, if you stood in the path of the waves, there would be four wave crests hitting you every second. If you were producing water waves by pushing the water surface down-and-then-up-again you would have to do the entire operation four times every second to generate waves having a frequency of 4 per second. We can express frequency in terms of the number of waves per second, and so have a unit of per second, i.e., s^{-1}, or hertz (Hz). One hertz is a frequency of one complete wave per second.

Waves also have a speed. Suppose the speed were 3 m per second, then this would be the speed at which we would see a crest, or a trough, apparently moving over the surface of the water. When a crest is produced then in one second it must move 3 m. If, in any second, 6 waves are produced then the first of the waves will have travelled a distance of 3 m from the source during the time that the 6 waves are produced. Thus the 6 waves are spread out over a distance of 3 m. The wavelength must therefore be 3/6, i.e., 0·5 m.

If the frequency is f, then f waves are produced in a second. If the wavelength of the waves is λ then, in 1 s, the wave must have covered a distance of $f \times \lambda$. The distance covered per second is the speed, hence the speed v must be given by

$$v = f\lambda$$

If the frequency of a wave is 5 Hz and its wavelength 0·2 m, then its speed must be

$$v = f\lambda = 5 \times 0\cdot2 = 1\cdot0 \text{ m/s}$$

If a frog hops 50 times a minute and each hop is of length 4 cm, its speed is the number of hops per unit time multiplied by the hop length, i.e., 200 cm/min.

It must be emphasized that the wave speed is not the speed of the corks floating on the surface of the water; the corks do not move forward with the wave. We see a wave moving with such and such a velocity, but the corks first bob up-and-down. It is like having a crowd of people and someone starts a whispered rumour in the middle of the crowd—the rumour spreads out from that person with a velocity but no person need move.

111

7.2 Reflection and refraction of waves

Figure 7.5 shows what happens when a drop of water is allowed to fall on the surface of a sheet of water. A pulse of waves is produced and these waves spread out from the impact point. Where the waves meet the barrier they are *reflected*, and we have a wave motion coming away from the barrier.

Figure 7.6 shows what happens when water waves pass from deep to shallow water. The direction of movement of the waves changes. This change in direction is called *refraction*. You may notice in the photograph that when the waves refract their wavelength changes.

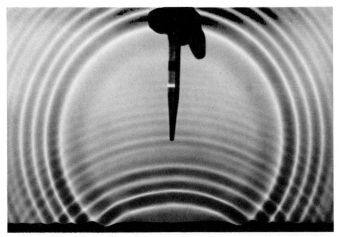

Fig. 7.5 (from *PSSC Physics*, *2nd edn*, courtesy D. C. Heath and Company, Lexington, Ma.)

Fig. 7.6 The waves are coming from the right (from *PSSC Physics*, *2nd edn*, D. C. Heath and Company, Lexington, Ma.)

7.3 Sound

When the lightning flashes the sound of thunder follows after a short interval of time. The nearer you are to the source of the lightning the shorter is the time interval between seeing the lightning and hearing the thunder. It is a common practice to count the seconds between seeing the flash and hearing the thunder, and to reckon that for every second the storm is about a third of a kilometre away. Sound thus travels with a definite speed in air.

If you shout in front of a large building or cliff you might hear an echo. The sound you produce is followed a little while later by the sound coming back to you, having been reflected from some distant object. The best reflectors for this purpose are large flat surfaces. We can measure the speed of sound by measuring the time taken for an echo to come back from a distant reflector. The source of the sound needs to be one which produces a short sharp sound, two iron bars being knocked together is suitable. If this is done in front of a large flat surface, the front of a building perhaps, then the time taken for the echo to return to the source position can be measured. The distance travelled during that time interval is the distance from the source to the reflector and back again. This needs to be measured. The speed is then the distance travelled divided by the time taken. Such measurements, and other types, lead to the result that sound travels in air, under normal conditions, at about 340 m/s.

The echo sounder used on board ship to determine the water depth works on the same principle, a measurement of the time taken for a pulse of sound to travel from the ship to the sea bed and back again. The speed of sound in sea water is different from that in air, the value being about 1500 m/s.

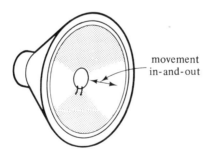

movement
in-and-out

Fig. 7.7

The speed of sound depends on the medium in which it is travelling. Sound, however, cannot travel through a vacuum. Experiments in which an electric bell is made to operate in a vacuum show that no sound is heard. The bell arm may be beating against the bell but no sound is transmitted.

Sound is produced by something moving, something moving backwards-and-forwards or up-and-down. It could be the vibrating string of a musical instrument or the vibrating cone of a loudspeaker; Fig. 7.7. Look around you at the sources of sound and you will see that the sources always oscillate.

113

But such a movement backwards-and-forwards must push and pull against the air. When you yourself jump forwards, you compress the air in front of you, for a short time. When you leap backwards the air in front of you expands. The forwards motion increases the air pressure, the backwards motion decreases the pressure in front of the moving object. A vibrating object, therefore, must be continually producing first an increase in pressure, then a reduction in pressure, then an increase, then a decrease, and so on. A patch of air must be first pushed forwards, then pulled backwards, then forwards again, then backwards, and so on. The patch of air is moving in a similar way to the cork on the water surface when a wave passes. The evidence suggests that sound is a wave motion.

The speed of sound in air depends on the air temperature, increasing as the temperature increases. Because the speed is different for different air temperatures, the wavelength must be different (the wavelength is proportional to the speed, $v = f\lambda$). We can have the situation where the air close to the ground is at a lower temperature than the air higher up, e.g., just after sunset. The wavelength of the sound in the air close to the ground will thus be smaller than that in the air higher up, and the sound waves bend towards the earth under such conditions; Fig. 7.8. When this happens, distant sounds can be heard, which under normal conditions would be inaudible.

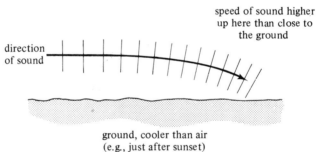

speed of sound higher
up here than close to
the ground

direction
of sound

ground, cooler than air
(e.g., just after sunset)

Fig. 7.8

7.4 Light

That light can be reflected is an everyday experience, familiar to you every time you look in a mirror. If you direct a beam of light at a mirror, the reflected beam of light can be detected; Fig. 7.9. The angle at which the reflected beam comes off the mirror depends on the angle with which the incident beam strikes the mirror. If you measure these angles, in an experiment, you will find that the angle at which the light reflects from the mirror always equals the angle with which the light is incident on the mirror. The convention is adopted of measuring the angles from the normal to the mirror at the point of incidence, and calling such angles the angle of incidence and the angle of reflection; Fig. 7.10. There is another law governing reflection: the reflected ray, the normal, and the incident ray are always in the same plane.

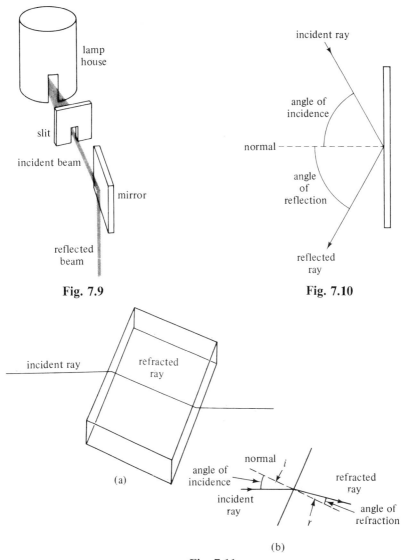

Fig. 7.9

Fig. 7.10

Fig. 7.11

If you try an experiment where you direct a beam of light on to a glass block, you will find that the light on passing from the air into the glass changes direction, i.e., light is refracted; Fig. 7.11. The relationship between the angle of incidence and the angle of refraction is not so obvious; it is that the sine of the angle of incidence divided by the sine of the angle of refraction is a constant:

$$\frac{\sin i}{\sin r} = \text{constant}$$

The constant depends on which two media are involved, e.g., in this example air to glass. The constant is called the *refractive index*. The incident ray, the normal, and the refracted ray all lie in the same plane.

Lenses are applications of this refraction of light. Lenses employ the bending of light to enable beams of light to be all brought to one point, i.e., focused, or made to diverge; Fig. 7.12. Lenses are generally made of glass, and the angle at which a beam of light emerges from the lens is governed by the angle at which the beam of light is incident on the glass surface of the lens. By changing the shape of this surface, different lenses can be produced which bend light rays differently. A lens which bends an incident parallel set of rays so that they all converge to one point is called a converging or convex lens. A lens which bends an incident parallel set of rays so that they all diverge is

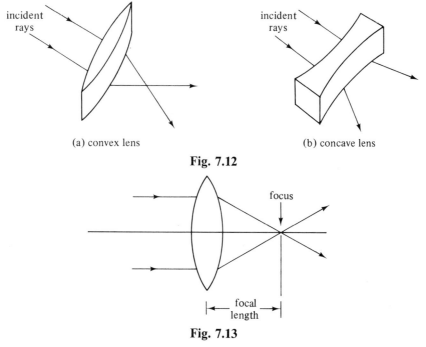

(a) convex lens   (b) concave lens

Fig. 7.12

Fig. 7.13

called a diverging or concave lens. In the case of the convex lens, the distance from the point at which the parallel rays converge to the centre of the lens is called the focal length; the point at which the rays all meet is the focus; Fig. 7.13. With a concave lens all the rays seem to diverge from some point. This point is called the focus, and its distance from the centre of the lens is called the focal length.

When you look into a mirror you see an image of yourself. If you lift your right hand the image in the mirror lifts its left hand. How can this effect be explained? What are images? The light starting at the object travels to the mirror, and then is reflected and so reaches your eye. The eye thus sees the object by rays of light that have been bent by the mirror; Fig. 7.14.

116

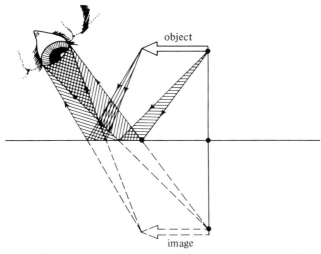

Fig. 7.14 (from *Patterns in Physics*, W. Bolton, McGraw-Hill, 1974)

The object seen by bent rays of light is what we call the image. Because we automatically think of light as travelling in straight lines then the object, or rather the image, seems to be behind the mirror. No light actually goes through the mirror to the image, it is what is called a virtual image.

A convex lens can be used to produce an image of some distant object. Essentially, this is what you do every time you use a camera to take a photograph. The rays of light from the distant object are bent by the lens in such a way as to give an image on the film in the camera; Fig. 7.15. This type of image is called a real image because the light actually does go to the image.

Light can be reflected and refracted; waves can be reflected and refracted. The conclusion on this might be that light is a wave motion. A stream of particles, however, can be reflected. If you throw a ball at a wall it bounces back—the bounce back might be called reflection of the ball. A stream of particles can be refracted. If a ball rolls down one slope and on to another slope of different incline its direction of motion changes—it refracts. All we

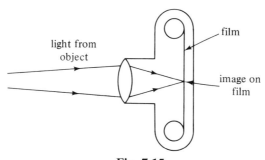

Fig. 7.15

117

can say is that, on the evidence we have so far, light could be a wave motion but the evidence is not conclusive.

Problems

What are waves?

1. A student uses a piece of wood to push down-and-then-up on the surface of water in a tank (Fig. 7.16), and he repeats this motion at the rate of five times a second. The waves so produced have their crest-to-crest distance measured as 0·10 m.
   (a) What is the frequency of the wave motion?
   (b) What is the wavelength of the wave?
   (c) What is the speed of the wave motion?
2. A wave has a frequency of 20 Hz and a wavelength of 1 mm. What is its speed?
3. When a wave is produced on a water surface what is it that travels? The wave? The water? Both wave and water?
4. Draw a diagram showing the pattern of crests and troughs produced, on a water surface, by a small disturbance at a point on the surface, e.g., a drop of water falling on to the water surface.

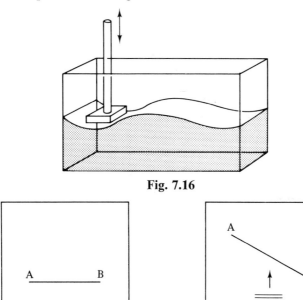

Fig. 7.16

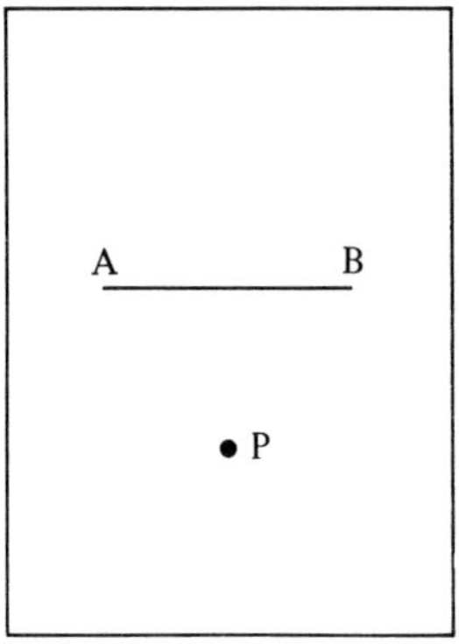

Fig. 7.17 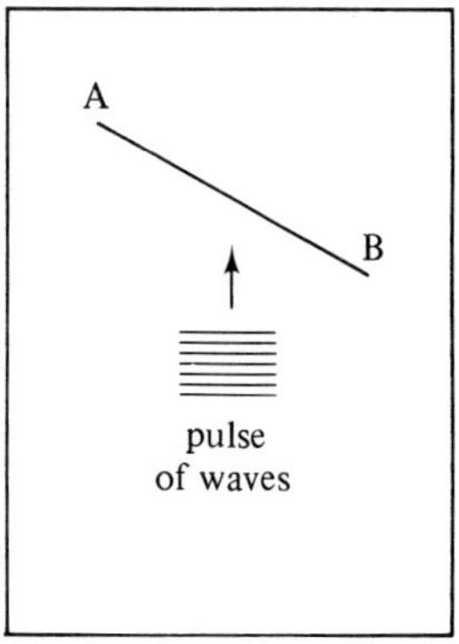   **Fig. 7.18**

Reflection and refraction of waves

5. Figure 7.17 shows a tray of water with the line AB representing a straight barrier. A pulse of waves is started at point P by dropping a drop of water on to the water surface.
   (a) Draw a diagram showing the pattern of crests and troughs a short enough time after the start of the pulse for the waves not to have reached the barrier.
   (b) Draw a diagram showing the wave pulse after the waves have reached the barrier.

6. Figure 7.18 shows a tray of water with the line AB representing a straight barrier. A pulse of straight crest waves is produced, and travels towards the barrier. The diagram shows this pulse sometime before the barrier is reached. Sketch the wave pulse after reflection from the barrier.

7. (a) How would you expect the wavelength of water waves to change as they move up a gently shelving beach?
   (b) How would you expect the speed of such waves to change?

8. Figure 7.19 shows a tray of water with the line AB representing a change in depth, such that waves coming from the lower side move from deep to shallow water. Sketch the straight crest wave pulse shown approaching AB as it crosses AB.

9. Figure 7.20 shows a tray of water with the shaded area being an area of water shallower than the rest of the water in the tray. Straight waves are shown approaching this area. What will be the form of the waves after they pass the shallow region?

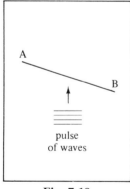

Fig. 7.19

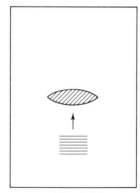

Fig. 7.20

Sound

10. An echo is found to occur 2 s after the production of the initial sound. How far away must be the object responsible for the echo? Take the speed of sound to be 340 m/s.

11. The speed of sound in sea water is 1500 m/s. A pulse of sound is produced at a ship and, after reflection at the sea bed, arrives back at the ship half a second later. How deep is the sea at that point?

119

12. The time interval between seeing the lightning flash and hearing the thunder is measured as being 7 s. How far away is the storm responsible for the lightning and the thunder? Take the speed of sound in air to be 340 m/s.
13. A loudspeaker produces sound with a frequency of 500 Hz. If the speed of sound is taken as 340 m/s, what will be the wavelength of the sound?
14. Why do tape recordings of voices sound 'wrong' when the tape is run at the 'wrong' speed? How would you expect the voices to change if the recording is played faster than the speed at which it was recorded?

Light
15. A point source of light, i.e., a very small source of light, produces sharp shadows of objects. Why does this suggest that light travels in straight lines?

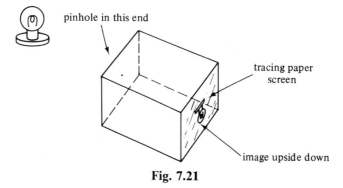

Fig. 7.21

16. A pin-hole camera is just a closed box with a pin-hole at one end and the sensitive film at the other end; Fig. 7.21. If you want to see how such a camera works you could make one out of a cardboard box and cover the film end with a sheet of tracing paper, this will enable you to see on this the image of the object being 'photographed'. The image with such a camera is an upside-down version of the object. Use the idea of light travelling in straight lines to explain this.
17. Why, when you look into a plane mirror, do you see an image of yourself apparently behind the mirror?
18. When a stick standing half in and half out of water is viewed it seems bent though it is in reality straight. Why is this so?

120

8. Chemical reactions

8.1 Air and burning

If we put a candle on a watch glass and allow the candle to burn, the candle will go on burning until all the candle has been used up. But, if we put the candle on a watch glass, light the candle, and then put it under a beaker, the candle does not go on burning for long; Fig. 8.1. If we use a larger beaker for the experiment the candle burns for longer. If, when the candle under the beaker is just flickering and about to go out, we lift the beaker, the candle flares up again. The experiment might suggest that the candle is in some way using up air, or perhaps part of the air, in the beaker.

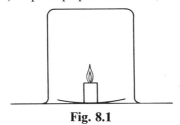

Fig. 8.1

If a piece of magnesium ribbon is ignited by a flame then the magnesium burns. Suppose, however, we do this ignition experiment more carefully and try to establish what is happening. We can put the magnesium ribbon in a crucible and cover it with a lid. The crucible and contents can then be weighed. Then the crucible and contents are heated. As we want to find out the part played by air during the burning, we need to lift the crucible lid to let in air during the burning, without losing any of the products of the burning. After the burning is complete, and the crucible has cooled down, weighing of the crucible and contents reveals that as a result of the burning the crucible and contents have gained in weight. The magnesium, as a result of burning, has increased in weight.

Suppose instead of using magnesium we use powdered copper. The copper as a result of heating to red heat gains in weight. If you do the experiment you will also no doubt notice that the copper after the experiment is no longer the 'normal' coppery colour, but is black. The magnesium after the burning is no longer the same shiny colour.

What is happening? A reasonable supposition is that as the burning seems to involve air and that as the magnesium and the copper gained weight, then they are taking something out of the air. Suppose we do the experiment

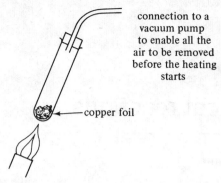

connection to a
vacuum pump
to enable all the
air to be removed
before the heating
starts

copper foil

Fig. 8.2 When heated in the absence of air no blackening of the copper occurs

with, say, the copper, and exclude air; Fig. 8.2. Will the copper turn black? Will it gain in weight? When such an experiment is done the copper does not turn black and does not gain in weight. For the copper to be blackened, and gain in weight, air is necessary. But is the copper using up the air when it turns black? To investigate this we need to measure the amount of air in a vessel containing copper, both before and after the copper has turned black. Figure 8.3 shows one way of doing this with a syringe. For every 100 cm³ of air present before heating about 20 cm³ are used up when the copper turns black. Copper turning black thus seems to involve the copper taking something out of the air. The 'air' that is left after the copper has extracted its part will not support burning. A burning taper put into this 'air' goes out immediately.

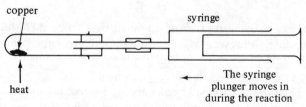

copper

syringe

heat

The syringe
plunger moves in
during the reaction

Fig. 8.3

Air appears to have an *active* and an *inactive* part. The active part allows burning, the inactive part does not. The active part is what we call oxygen, the inactive part is predominantly the gas called nitrogen. The black substance formed by the interaction of the copper and oxygen is called copper oxide. Oxides are the names of the substances formed when an element interacts with oxygen to give a compound. The experiment with the copper could have been done with steel wool, and would have resulted in the production of iron oxide. The iron combines with the oxygen in the air to give the oxide.

When coal burns the reaction is similar to that described above for copper. Coal contains predominantly the element carbon. The carbon combines with the oxygen in the air to form an oxide of carbon. Oxygen is needed for the reaction.

8.2 Compounds

An oxide is the compound formed when an element reacts with oxygen. Common salt is a compound formed of sodium and chlorine and called sodium chloride. Copper with chlorine gives copper chloride. Chlorides are the compounds in which chlorine is combined with an element. Compounds are formed when we combine two or more elements together.

How can we tell what elements have combined to give a compound? The most obvious ways are either to make the compound by allowing the elements to react together, or breaking up a compound to yield its constituent elements. We might for an example consider the compound water. What are the constituent elements of water?

In the experiment with the candle burning under a beaker (Fig. 8.1) you might have observed that condensation appears on the inside of the beaker during the burning of the candle. The condensation is water. When copper was heated in air an oxide, copper oxide, was produced. Is water an oxide, a combination of oxygen with some other substance?

If water is an oxide, then it might be possible to get the oxygen in the water to combine with some metal and so produce an oxide of that metal. Figure 8.4 is one way such an experiment can be tried. The iron filings in the test tube are heated, and also the water in the asbestos is heated. The iron forms an oxide, and a gas is produced which can be collected by allowing it to bubble through the water into a test tube. If the flame of a match is brought up to the mouth of the test tube containing this gas there is a bang. The gas is not oxygen. This inflammable gas is called hydrogen.

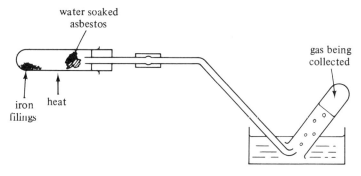

Fig. 8.4

Water is a compound formed between oxygen and hydrogen. You might call it hydrogen oxide.

The compounds of elements are given names which end in -*ide*. For example, hydrogen oxide, sodium chloride. Compounds of three elements usually contain oxygen and the commonest tend to have names ending in -*ate*, e.g., sodium chlorate (sodium, chlorine, and oxygen), copper sulphate (copper, sulphur, and oxygen).

123

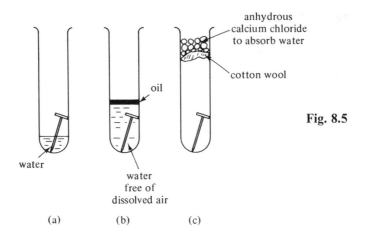

anhydrous
calcium chloride
to absorb water

cotton wool

oil

Fig. 8.5

water

water
free of
dissolved air

(a)   (b)   (c)

8.3 Rusting

Iron and steel objects, perhaps a bicycle or a car, tend to rust when left outside a great deal. Iron and steel objects indoors do not seem to rust, at least not so readily. This would seem to suggest that water may be involved in the rusting process. Damp conditions seem to lead to rusting. The oxygen from the air might also be an active agent. One way of investigating these factors might be to put into one test tube a bright iron nail, and just a little water; Fig. 8.5. In a second test tube an identical nail is placed, but the nail is completely immersed in water (the water should have been boiled so that all the dissolved air is removed). In a third test tube another nail is put, but this time the open end of the tube is plugged with cotton wool and some anhydrous calcium chloride. This substance absorbs water and so keeps the air in the test tube dry. It would seem that with the three test tubes we have the following conditions:

1. water and air present;
2. only water present (to stop air entering the water a layer of oil can be put on the water surface);
3. air only.

The result of such an investigation is that the iron exposed to both the water and air rusts, but with only either the air or water present there is no rusting. To prevent rusting then we must keep water and air away from the iron.

Painting is one way of stopping air and water coming into contact with iron or steel. Plating with tin or chromium is another way. Chromium-plated car bumpers and tin-plated steel for canned food are examples of this. Coating with plastics, for example objects such as a dish draining rack for use in the kitchen, is another way of preventing the iron coming into contact with air and water. Look around you and consider the various ways that are used to prevent the development of rust.

In 1913 Harry Brearly was experimenting with mixing substances together to produce different alloys based on iron. The aim was to find a good steel for gun barrels. Among the many samples that he rejected was one containing about 14 per cent chromium. Some months later he noticed that in the pile of rejected test pieces this chromium steel was still bright and shiny while the other steels were rusty. This chromium steel is what we now call stainless steel. It is far more rust resistant than other steels or iron.

8.4 Conduction of electricity

If you take a battery and connect it by means of copper wires to an ammeter, then the meter shows a current. Instead of the meter we could have a torch bulb, the bulb lights when the connecting wires are made of copper. In fact, we can get currents when we use metals for the conducting wires. Metals are good conductors of electricity. If we tried to use glass rod for the connections between the battery and the meter then no current would be detected. With glass rod for the connections to the torch bulb we would get no light from the bulb. Glass is an insulator, i.e., a bad conductor of electricity.

Suppose we connect a battery via copper leads and an ammeter to a beaker containing distilled (pure) water; Fig. 8.6. Is water a good or bad conductor of electricity? Distilled water is a bad conductor of electricity. Suppose, however, we add common salt to the water so that we have a salt solution, then conduction of electricity occurs. A solution of common salt in water is a good conductor of electricity. If we tried a block of common salt we would find that it is not a good conductor of electricity. Dissolving the common salt in water makes two bad conductors into a good conductor of electricity. Observation of the solution while it is conducting electricity discloses that some decomposition is occurring—gas is being produced.

Suppose we repeat the experiment, but this time use a solution of copper sulphate in water. The solution is a good conductor of electricity. Decomposition again occurs while there is a current. This time the decomposition shows itself as a loss in copper from one of the copper wires dipping into the solution, and a gain in copper of the other wire. If this wire has a metal object, perhaps a coin, attached to its end then the object becomes copper plated. The copper is always deposited on the wire connected to the negative side of the battery, the wire connected to the positive side being the one that loses copper; Fig. 8.7(a). This is the basis of the process of electro-plating.

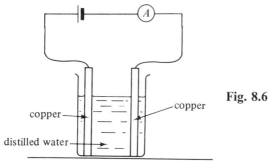

Fig. 8.6

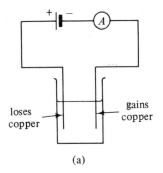

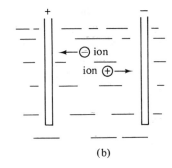

(a)   **Fig. 8.7**   (b)

It would seem that the break-up of a compound is necessary for the electrical conduction to occur. Dissolving a compound in water must somehow break a compound into pieces. The pieces are called *ions*. The compound is considered, initially, to be made up of positively and negatively charged parts which attract each other and so keep the compound together. When the compound is put in water these two parts separate to give positive and negative ions. When the battery is connected to wires dipping into the solution, then the positive ion is attracted to the wire connected to the negative side of the battery, and the negative ion moves to the wire that is connected to the positive side of the battery; Fig. 8.7(b). The movement of the ions is what constitutes the electric current through the solution.

The strips of metal dipping into the solution are called *electrodes*, the solution that allows the conduction is called the *electrolyte*, and the entire process is called *electrolysis*.

8.5 Electricity from chemical reactions

When a current passes through a solution, such as sodium chloride in water, a chemical change occurs. Can a chemical change be used to produce electricity? Figure 8.8 shows an arrangement which does just this. It consists of a piece of copper and a piece of zinc dipping into a beaker containing sodium chloride dissolved in water, the pieces of the metals being connected by leads to a milliammeter. A current flows. Other metals can be tried; the result is that a current flows only when two different metals are used in the circuit. No current is produced if both strips are made of the same metal. Some pairs of metals are better than others at behaving as a battery. If we take copper as one of the strips and then try different metals for the other strip we can arrive at a table something like:

> magnesium
> aluminium
> zinc
> iron
> tin
> lead
> copper

126

The further away from copper the other metal appears in the table, then the greater the voltage of the battery produced. Thus magnesium and copper are better than zinc and copper. Zinc and copper are better than lead and copper, etc. Combinations of two metals other than copper can be used, but whichever two are used, the further apart they are in the table then the greater is the voltage produced. Also, the metal which is highest in the list is always the positive terminal. So for the copper–zinc arrangement the zinc is the positive terminal, and the copper the negative terminal.

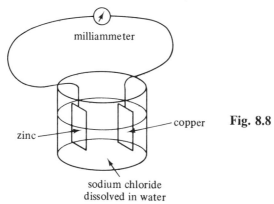

milliammeter

zinc

copper **Fig. 8.8**

sodium chloride
dissolved in water

8.6 Reactivity with oxygen

Suppose we heat equal parts of magnesium powder with dry copper oxide. What might happen? The magnesium could take the oxygen from the copper to give magnesium oxide and copper, or the copper could keep hold of its oxygen and deny it to the magnesium. Great care is needed in performing this experiment, because a violent reaction occurs—magnesium does take the oxygen from copper.

Suppose we try equal parts of magnesium and dry lead oxide. On heating a violent reaction occurs. The magnesium takes the oxygen from the lead.

Suppose we try iron filings with zinc oxide. On heating no reaction occurs. The iron does not take the oxygen from the zinc. If we try iron filings with copper oxide a reaction does occur. The iron does take the oxygen from the copper.

We can try a whole group of experiments with elements and oxides, seeing which element is able to take the oxygen from a particular oxide. The results of these experiments can be expressed in a simple table, all the results conforming to the same pattern:

magnesium
aluminium
zinc
iron
tin
lead
copper

127

To read the table add (in imagination) the word oxide after all the elements other than the element in the experiment. If the element is higher up the table than the element forming the oxide, then it will take the oxygen from the oxide. If the element is lower in the table than the element forming the oxide, then it will not take the oxygen from the oxide. Thus, for example, aluminium would take the oxygen from an oxide of tin, but could not take the oxygen from an oxide of magnesium.

This pattern was the same as the pattern found when we tried different metals together to obtain electricity.

Water is an oxide, hydrogen oxide, and so we can determine the place of hydrogen in the above table by finding out which of the above metals will take the oxygen from water. Hydrogen comes between copper and lead. Thus magnesium will take oxygen from water (in the form of steam), copper will not.

➘ 8.7 Extraction of metals from their ores

Iron exists in nature in the form of compounds, often iron oxide. To obtain the iron alone the oxygen has to be removed from the oxide. This could be done by heating the oxide with a metal that appears higher up the list than iron, e.g., aluminium or magnesium. However, since large quantities of aluminium or magnesium would be needed, the process would be very expensive. In practice, the iron oxide is heated with carbon; the carbon removes the oxygen from the iron ore.

8.8 Corrosion

When an electric current passes between two copper electrodes dipping in copper sulphate solution, then one of the electrodes becomes worn away as it loses copper. The other electrode gains copper. If we have two different metals for the electrodes and they dip into a solution which allows conduction, then we have a *cell* and electricity is produced. If we consider both the effects occurring together we have the basis of an explanation of corrosion. Corrosion is the gradual destruction of a metal, the gradual wasting away of a metal, in the presence of a damp atmosphere.

Rusting of iron occurs in the presence of water and oxygen, i.e., a damp atmosphere. This is an example of what we call corrosion. A piece of metal, such as iron, in contact with moisture behaves like a small cell and produces localized currents. These currents remove metal from one region and put it in another. The piece of iron can behave like two different metals, a necessary condition for a cell to be produced, because it is not normally uniformly iron, but impurities present in the iron lead to sufficient variations for the cell to be produced. There are other ways in which the iron can behave like two different metals and give a cell, the net effect is however the same. The iron in the process of moving between electrodes picks up oxygen and forms the compound we call rust. Thus the result of the cell action is a current which moves iron and allows it to combine with oxygen. Both oxygen and water are necessary for rusting to occur.

When electrolysis occurs it is the electrode which is connected to the positive side of the battery that always becomes thinner as it loses material. One way of stopping this corrosion of iron is to make it the negative electrode. To do this for a wet sheet of iron means providing some other material which, when it forms a battery with the iron, will become the positive electrode and leave the iron to be the negative electrode. The pattern of elements we looked at earlier shows that this can be done if we take a material which is higher up the list than iron. Zinc is such a material. Putting a layer of zinc on iron thus gives protection to the iron against corrosion. This composite material is known as galvanized iron.

8.9 Acids and alkalis

You may have taken a powder to cure an 'acid stomach'. If you had examined the packet from which the powder came you might have found that the main ingredient was magnesium hydroxide. The effect of the powder seems to be to remove the *acidity*. You might have come across chemicals called acids, or possibly the sweets called acid drops. What would happen if magnesium hydroxide was added to such acids? You could try the experiment with an acid drop, taste it, and then see how the taste changes when magnesium hydroxide is added. The acid taste is removed.

If you crush rose petals, or perhaps a piece of beetroot, or a coloured natural substance, and then dissolve the crushed substance in a mixture of alcohol and water you can produce an indicator which will distinguish between substances like acid drops and magnesium hydroxide. In the laboratory you may use litmus as an indicator. This is just a processed extract of lichen, a naturally occurring substance. You may come across other indicators. They all have the property of changing colour, with the resulting colour depending on the degree of acidity or alkalinity of the substance they are put in contact with. Acids turn litmus red, alkalis turn litmus blue. An indicator called a universal indicator is a mixture of indicators which can show as many as six distinctly different colours with solutions varying from very acidic to very alkaline. Sodium bicarbonate is an example of an alkali, but is only slightly alkaline. To distinguish the slightly alkaline from the very alkaline, the slightly acidic from the very acidic, a scale is used called the pH scale. The part of the scale most used runs from pH 0 to pH 14.

very acidic	pH 2 and lower
slightly acidic	pH 5, approximately
neutral	pH 7
slightly alkaline	pH 9, approximately
very alkaline	pH 12 and higher

A typical universal indicator might give the following colours:

purple	above pH 12
blue	pH 10
green	pH 8
yellow	pH 6
orange	pH 4
pink	pH 2
red	pH 1 and lower

Pure water has a pH of 7, i.e., it is neutral. If the pH of the magnesium hydroxide in solution is measured, a value of perhaps pH 9 might be obtained. A solution made by dissolving the acid drop sweet in water might have a value of about pH 5. By mixing the two solutions in the right proportions we can obtain a resulting solution with pH 7, i.e., a neutral solution. Curing the acidic stomach means changing the pH to give a value of about pH 7 corresponding to the neutral situation.

The digestive juices in the stomach contain an acid called hydrochloric acid and this is, as the name implies, acidic. Certain types of indigestion are produced by the juices becoming too acidic. The indigestion powders are alkaline and are used to neutralize the acid.

When an acid reacts with an alkali a compound is produced to which we give the name *salt*. For example, hydrochloric acid reacts with sodium hydroxide to give a salt, sodium chloride, and water. Sulphuric acid reacts with sodium hydroxide to give a salt, sodium sulphate, and water. Salts are substances like chlorides and sulphates. They are prepared by neutralizing an acid.

8.10 Chemical equations

Hydrochloric acid reacts with sodium hydroxide to give sodium chloride and water. We can write this as an equation:

hydrochloric acid + sodium hydroxide = sodium chloride + water

Hydrochloric acid is a compound of the elements hydrogen and chlorine. Sodium hydroxide is a compound involving the elements sodium, oxygen, and hydrogen. Sodium chloride involves sodium and chlorine, and water is a compound of hydrogen and oxygen. We could thus write our equation in terms of the elements in each compound.

hydrogen with chlorine	+	sodium with oxygen and hydrogen	=	sodium with chlorine	+	hydrogen with oxygen

On the left-hand side of the equation we have the elements hydrogen, chlorine, sodium, and oxygen. On the right-hand side of the equation we have hydrogen, chlorine, sodium, and oxygen. The same *elements* occur on each

130

side of the equation. The same *compounds* do not occur on each side of the equation.

Sulphuric acid reacts with sodium hydroxide to give sodium sulphate and water. This reaction can be written as:

sulphuric acid + sodium hydroxide = sodium sulphate + water

or in terms of the elements:

hydrogen	sodium	sodium	
with	with	with	hydrogen
sulphur	+ oxygen	= sulphur	+ with
and	and	and	oxygen
oxygen	hydrogen	oxygen	

On the left-hand side of the equation we have the elements hydrogen, sulphur, oxygen, sodium, and the right-hand side has hydrogen, sulphur, oxygen, sodium.

8.11 Ions

Hydrogen chloride can be made by burning hydrogen in chlorine; both hydrogen and chlorine are gases and the product hydrogen chloride is a gas. If the hydrogen chloride gas is tested with an indicator there is little if any change, provided the gas and the indicator are not wet. If there is water present then the indicator shows an acid to be present. Hydrogen chloride gas dissolved in water gives what is called hydrochloric acid. Water seems to be an essential part of the acid. But, as electrolysis has shown, water breaks down molecules into ions. Ions thus seem to be an essential part of being acidic. But what ions? Any ion? All the acids are hydrogen compounds, e.g., hydrochloric acid is hydrogen with chlorine, sulphuric acid is hydrogen with sulphur and oxygen, nitric acid is hydrogen with nitrogen and oxygen.

Electrolysis of a strong solution of hydrogen chloride in water produces hydrogen at the negative electrode and chlorine at the positive electrode. The hydrogen ions are thus positive ions. An acid can thus be described as a compound which yields hydrogen ions.

What about alkalis? Hydrochloric acid with sodium hydroxide gives sodium chloride plus water. We have the acid supplying hydrogen ions. As the reaction produces water you might suspect that the sodium hydroxide supplies the other ion to make the hydrogen ion into water. Water is made up of two hydrogen atoms and one oxygen atom. The sodium hydroxide supplies an hydroxide ion, a charged bundle made up of an oxygen and a hydrogen atom. The hydroxide ion is negatively charged and this ion together with the positive hydrogen ion makes up a water molecule. Alkalis are soluble compounds that yield hydroxide ions.

When sodium chloride, common salt, is dissolved in water we would expect there to be sodium ions and chlorine ions produced. But free sodium is extremely reactive and would react with the water. Chlorine is a gas, a poisonous gas, and should therefore escape from the water. But these things

131

do not happen. When we consider the sodium reacting with the water, or the chlorine escaping as a gas, we are considering atoms, and the properties of atoms are different from the properties of the same substances when existing as ions. Water contains hydrogen ions, but the hydrogen does not escape from the water until we supply charge which converts the ions into atoms. We have to supply electrons, from a battery, to convert the positive ions into neutral atoms—the result is called electrolysis.

8.12 Patterns

The pattern encountered in this chapter is called the electrochemical series. The pattern enables forecasts to be made not only of the reactions of the substances with oxygen to form oxides, but also on how pairs of the elements of the series will behave when used to make a battery. These have the same pattern because, in both cases, we really are concerned with the ease with which the elements form ions.

When a battery is made from electrodes of zinc and copper dipping into an electrolyte, the zinc is always the positive electrode and the copper the negative electrode. What we are saying is that the zinc more readily attracts negative ions than the copper. This would indicate that when the zinc is in the electrolyte it is more positive than the copper. Unlike charges attract each other, and the attraction is greater the greater the charges involved. Zinc forms positive ions more readily than copper. Our series can thus be written:

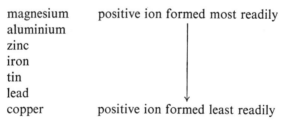

magnesium   positive ion formed most readily
aluminium
zinc
iron
tin
lead
copper   positive ion formed least readily

This explains the reactivity of the elements with oxygen. The oxygen in an oxide can be pulled away from its metal element by a more positively charged metal element. If magnesium and tin compete for oxygen, then the magnesium will win because it forms positive ions more readily.

We can relate this ease of forming positive ions to the structure of the atoms of the elements. There is a grander pattern of which this electrochemical series is just a small part. We could have looked at other patterns, this chapter, however, has been limited to the area which is most likely to be of interest to you at this level.

Problems

Air and burning

1. We need to breathe oxygen to live. How could you test if there was oxygen present in an enclosure without trying to live in it?

2. In a building on fire people may die of suffocation rather than burns. How is it possible for them to die from lack of oxygen?

3. How could you explain to a fellow student the reason why, in an experiment involving heating copper in air, the copper weighs more after the experiment than before?

Compounds

4. We can have oxides formed by many elements, e.g., copper oxide, aluminium oxide, iron oxide. What have all the compounds in common?

5. Sodium chloride is a compound formed between the elements sodium and chlorine. What are the elements which form barium chloride?

Rusting

6. How does painting an iron object reduce the chances of rust occurring?

7. Iron objects covered with a layer of grease or oil do not rust. Why not?

Conduction of electricity

8. How would you set about copper-plating a piece of metal?

9. Why should there be no electric points near a sink in a kitchen or in a bathroom?

Electricity from chemical reactions

10. If you made a cell with electrodes of zinc and lead, which would be the positive electrode and which the negative one?

11. Which cell would give the higher voltage, a magnesium–iron cell or a magnesium–copper cell?

Reactivity with oxygen

12. In which of the following might you expect a reaction to occur when the mixture is heated?
    (a) Magnesium oxide and copper.
    (b) Magnesium and copper oxide.
    (c) Iron oxide and tin.
    (d) Lead oxide and zinc.

Extraction of metals from their ores

13. A very early method of producing iron involved heating the iron ore in a charcoal fire. When the fire died down a spongy mass of rather impure iron remained. Explain the type of reaction that was occurring.

14. The reactivity table of elements can be increased to take on other elements. The lower end of the table can be increased as follows:

    tin
    lead
    copper
    silver
    gold

133

Gold and silver occur in nature in the metallic form. Copper occasionally appears as lumps of copper metal. The higher elements however appear as compounds, often oxides. Why do you think this is so?

Corrosion

15. Why does iron not rust in the absence of water?
16. Why do you think a pure metal would be likely to resist corrosion better than an impure metal?
17. Corrosion often occurs around welds and rivets in a structure. Why does it occur at these places rather than in the main body of the metal in the structure?

Acids and alkalis

18. How could you test a liquid to ascertain whether it was acidic or alkaline?
19. A solution is found to have a pH of 9. Is the solution acidic or alkaline?

Chemical equations

20. Iron oxide + carbon = iron + ?
    What must be the elements completing the above equation?
21. Calcium oxide + water = ?
    What must be the elements on the right-hand side of the equation?
22. Copper heated in the presence of oxygen gives copper oxide. Express this reaction in the form of an equation which shows the elements of the various substances involved.

Ions

23. Explain what happens to hydrogen chloride gas when it dissolves in water. Use the word ion in your explanation.

Discussion points

1. Iron was originally produced by the use of charcoal and so ready access to forests was necessary. Later coke became used in place of charcoal, so access to forests was no longer necessary. The iron industry was then located in different places. What factors now determine where the iron industry should be located?
2. Sometimes, on a long bridge, there is a team of workmen continually painting it, and when they reach the far end of the bridge it is always time to restart painting at the near end again. Corrosion of iron and steel is an expensive process. How does corrosion have to be taken into account in the design of a building or a bridge? How does it affect the running costs of a structure once it has been built?

Background reading

Nuffield Chemistry Background Books, Longmans/Penguin, 1966.
(a) *Chemicals and where they come from*
(b) *Burning*

Index

135

Typeset by John Wright & Sons Ltd., Bristol 4. Printed by J. W. Arrowsmith Ltd., Bristol.